let's do Brunch

recipes BRIGIT BINNS

photographs RAY KACHATORIAN

weldon**owen**

introduction

I was introduced to the concept of long Sunday brunches in New York City—home to some of the country's most enthusiastic brunchers! This unique-in-the-week meal is enjoyed far from the rigors of strict weekday schedules, and that fact alone makes it feel special.

Brunch can be herbal tea (or mimosas) and soft-scrambled eggs at eleven o'clock in the morning; an array of fresh juices with a spiral-cut ham, buttermilk biscuits, and a crumbly-sweet coffee cake at high noon; or a buffet with best friends bringing their favorite dishes that lasts all afternoon. This all-American invention showcases what we do best: innovation mixed with classicism wrapped in a comfortable, inclusive sensibility.

Nutritionists tell us that breakfast is the most important meal of the day, yet many of us continue to skip—or skimp on—this morning tradition, opting instead to grab something as we rush out the door. At brunch, where the luxury of time is built into the occasion, guests can relax as they work their way around a table of old favorites and new ideas—a mix of savory and sweet, of fruits and vegetables, of meats, cheeses, breads, and beverages.

Although brunch can be formal or informal, it is more often a relaxed gathering—a perfect time to introduce new people to one another, to gently mix families, or to reminisce with a coterie of old friends. It's a get-together that's defined by the host or hostess, not by tradition. That makes it one of the most fun and flexible ways to entertain, as well as one of the most satisfying meals to both serve and eat.

brunch entertaining

For me, a onetime overly ambitious hostess who is now wedded to the joys of make-ahead, brunch offers the possibility of a convivial meal that's light on preparation once the guests have arrived. When creating a menu, I am always careful to include only one dish that requires my last-minute attention, which allows me to join, and enjoy, the brunch. I plan dishes that match the season and the occasion, as well. Plus, brunch doesn't need to be a multicourse affair. Hosting can mean setting up a granola or bagel bar, where guests can choose their own toppings; passing platters of scrambled eggs and bacon at the table family-style; or composing a perfect plate of sweet and savory treats. Fresh fruit juices, coffee and tea, and a signature drink round out every menu. Here are a few of my general guidelines for brunch entertaining.

cook with the seasons
Keep the seasons in mind when planning your menu, both when selecting fresh ingredients in the market, such as asparagus in the spring and acorn squash in the fall, and when deciding what dishes best suit the time of year: summer days are great for lighter fare, like salads and frittatas, while chilly fall mornings call for comfort food such as polenta with poached eggs or huevos rancheros.

showcase fruit
Almost every brunch menu, no matter the time of year, calls for fruit, whether whole or in a salad and always as a juice—or even all three. Citrus and other fruit juices are a mainstay of my brunch table, providing refreshment, vitamins, and color—and often a partner for sparkling wine.

buffet-style ease
A brunch buffet frees the host or hostess from table service, allows guests to choose for themselves, and showcases the food and drink. For a crowd, make up two platters or bowls of each menu item and divide them between two stations, so no one will have to wait too long to fill his or her plate. For a granola bar, offer yogurt and milk along with bowls of dried fruits and nuts; for a bagel bar, include cream cheese, a variety of smoked fish, capers, and sliced tomatoes and onions.

serving strategies
To keep pancakes and waffles warm while you finish cooking the remaining batter, transfer them to a rack set over a baking sheet and put them in a preheated 200°F (95°C) oven until ready to serve. This method works for sausages and bacon, too.

juice bar
Place a bowlful of halved citrus on a kitchen island alongside an electric juicer or manual juice press so guests can squeeze their own glasses of fresh juice. Or, prepare or purchase freshly squeezed juices and serve in glass pitchers. Provide glasses, sparkling water, and ice cubes for spritzers.

sweet

sweet toppings

I like to set up a granola bar for brunch, with bowls of such toppings as fresh fruit, nuts, yogurt, and fragrant honey, and let guests create their ideal parfait.

honey butter

4 Tbsp (2 oz/60 g) unsalted butter, at room temperature

2 Tbsp good-quality honey

Kosher salt

In a bowl, combine the butter, honey, and salt to taste. Using a handheld mixer, beat together until creamy and fluffy, about 2 minutes. Store in the refrigerator, wrapped in plastic wrap, until ready to use.

makes about ¼ cup (2 oz/60 g)

fruit compote

2 cups (10 oz/315 g) peeled, pitted, and cut-up ripe, seasonal fruit, such as peaches, nectarines, plums, cherries, apples, pears, strawberries, blackberries, or rhubarb

2 tsp fresh lemon juice

About ¼ cup (2 oz/60 g) sugar, depending on the sweetness of the fruit

In a saucepan, combine the fruit, lemon juice, and sugar. Simmer over medium heat, stirring occasionally, until the fruit becomes juicy and is just tender. The timing will depend on the type of fruit. For example, you'll likely need to cook berries for only a few minutes, but apples or rhubarb will take longer to soften and release their juices. Remove from the heat and set aside to cool. Serve warm, or cover and refrigerate and serve chilled. The compote will keep for up to 1 week in the refrigerator.

makes about 2 cups (16 fl oz/500 ml)

raspberry jam

1 large Granny Smith apple

2 pt (1 lb/500 g) raspberries

1 cup (8 oz/250 g) sugar

2 Tbsp fresh lemon juice

Place a couple of saucers in the freezer to chill. Have ready a small stainless-steel bowl set in a bowl of ice water. Shred the apple, including the skin, on the large holes of a box grater; discard the core and seeds.

In a saucepan, combine the shredded apple, raspberries, sugar, and lemon juice. Bring to a boil over medium heat, stirring constantly to dissolve the sugar. Reduce the heat to medium-low and cook uncovered, stirring occasionally, until the berries break down and the juices thicken, about 10 minutes.

To test, remove a chilled saucer from the freezer. Spoon about 1 teaspoon of the berry mixture onto the saucer and let stand for 15 seconds. If the liquid thickens to a jamlike consistency, the jam is ready. If not, continue to cook for a few minutes longer and test again. Transfer the jam to the bowl set over ice water and let stand until cooled and thickened. Store in an airtight container in the refrigerator for up to 2 weeks.

makes about 2 cups (16 fl oz/500 ml)

whipped cream

1 cup (8 fl oz/250 ml) heavy cream

1 Tbsp sugar, or more to taste

1 tsp pure vanilla extract

In a bowl, combine the cream, sugar to taste, and vanilla. Using a handheld mixer, beat on medium-high speed until medium peaks form. Don't overwhip the cream, or it will become stiff and grainy. Serve right away, or cover and refrigerate for up to 2 hours. Fluff the cream with a whisk before serving.

makes about 2 cups (16 fl oz/500 ml)

lemon curd

1 large egg

4 large egg yolks

½ cup (4 oz/125 g) sugar

⅓ cup (3 fl oz/80 ml) fresh lemon juice

2 Tbsp unsalted butter

In a heatproof bowl set over (but not touching) barely simmering water in a saucepan, whisk together the whole egg, egg yolks, sugar, and lemon juice. Cook, stirring constantly, until thickened, about 5 minutes. Remove from the heat, add the butter, and stir until incorporated. Strain into another bowl. Cover with a piece of plastic wrap pressed directly on the surface of the curd and refrigerate until chilled. The curd will keep in the refrigerator for about 1 week.

makes about 1 cup (8 fl oz/250 ml)

banana–brown butter waffles with dulce de leche

Canola oil for cooking

1 cup (8 fl oz/250 ml) dulce de leche

2⅓ cups (20 fl oz/ 625 ml) whole milk, or as needed

4 Tbsp (2 oz/60 g) unsalted butter, plus more for serving

2 large eggs, separated

1 tsp pure vanilla extract

2 cups (10 oz/315 g) all-purpose flour

3 Tbsp sugar

4 tsp baking powder

¼ tsp salt

2 ripe bananas, peeled and thinly sliced

serves 4

Using a paper towel, lightly oil the grid of a waffle iron with canola oil, then preheat the iron.

In a small saucepan, heat the dulce de leche over medium heat, stirring frequently, until warm and melted. Gradually whisk in about ½ cup (4 fl oz/125 ml) of the milk, or enough to make a pourable sauce about the thickness of heavy cream. Remove from the heat, cover, and keep warm.

In another small saucepan, melt the 4 Tbsp butter over medium-low heat. Cook, stirring occasionally, until the milk solids in the bottom of the pan turn a toasty brown, about 3 minutes. Transfer to a bowl and let cool slightly. Add the remaining 2 cups (16 fl oz/ 500 ml) milk, the egg yolks, and the vanilla and whisk until combined.

In a large bowl, sift together the flour, sugar, baking powder, and salt. Add the milk mixture and whisk just until combined (a few lumps are okay). In another bowl, using an electric mixer, beat the egg whites on high speed until soft peaks form. Scatter the banana slices over the top. Scoop the egg whites over the batter and, using the whisk, gently and evenly fold in the whites and bananas.

Following the manufacturer's instructions, ladle some of the batter onto the grid of the waffle iron, close the lid, and cook until the waffle is golden brown and crisp and steam is no longer escaping from the sides of the iron. The timing will depend on the iron. Transfer to a plate and serve right away, or place on a baking sheet in a 200°F (95°C) oven for up to 20 minutes before serving. Repeat with the remaining batter, being careful not to stack the waffles on the sheet. Serve the waffles with the dulce de leche sauce and butter.

serve with

A jumble of blueberries jump-starts morning palates. Serve them in glass bowls and accompany with tumblers of unfiltered apple juice. Round out the brunch menu with a platter of Maple-Glazed Bacon (page 146); and if the occasion calls for a cocktail (as it frequently does), add a dash of dark rum and/or ginger beer to the apple juice.

The sweetness of milk, literally, dulce de leche, makes me smile in anticipation of this dish. These waffles are comforting and cozy—just as breakfast should be.

Here is French toast for grown-ups, with a coating of crisp nuts and the bright, racy pop of scarlet berries.

almond-crusted french toast with berries

6 large eggs

1 cup (8 fl oz/250 ml) half-and-half

2 Tbsp granulated sugar

Grated zest of 1 orange

¾ tsp almond extract (optional)

½ tsp pure vanilla extract

8 thick slices challah or other egg bread, preferably day-old

Canola oil for cooking

1 cup (4 oz/125 g) sliced almonds

1 cup (4 oz/125 g) raspberries

Confectioners' sugar or pure maple syrup for serving

serves 4

Preheat the oven to 350°F (180°C). Have ready 2 baking sheets.

In a large, shallow bowl, whisk together the eggs, half-and-half, granulated sugar, orange zest, almond extract (if using), and vanilla. Add the bread slices and turn gently to coat evenly. Let stand until the bread has soaked up some of the egg mixture, about 1 minute.

Heat a griddle over medium heat until hot. Lightly oil the griddle and one of the baking sheets. Spread the almonds on a plate. One piece at a time, remove the bread from the egg mixture, letting the excess liquid drip back into the bowl. Dip one side of the bread into the almonds, pressing gently to help the nuts adhere. Place on the ungreased baking sheet.

Place the bread slices on the griddle, almond side down, and cook until the nuts begin to brown, about 2 minutes. Turn and cook until golden brown on the second sides, about 2 minutes. Transfer to the greased baking sheet, almond side down, and bake until the center of the bread is heated through but still moist, about 10 minutes.

Serve the French toast topped with raspberries and dusted with confectioners' sugar or drizzled with maple syrup.

serve with

Put some greenery on the menu with Spring Vegetable Frittata (page 72), and add protein with a spiral-sliced glazed ham placed center stage on the buffet table. Wrap warm buttermilk biscuits in a linen towel and pack lightly salted cultured butter into a small crock, then set them both alongside the ham.

I love the way summery blueberries burst in my mouth like little purple balloons.

buttermilk blueberry pancakes

2 cups (10 oz/315 g) all-purpose (plain) flour

2 tsp baking powder

1 tsp baking soda

1 tsp salt

2 large eggs

2 cups (16 fl oz/ 500 ml) buttermilk

4 Tbsp (2 oz/60 g) unsalted butter, melted and cooled, plus more for brushing

1 pt (8 oz/250 g) blueberries

serves 6–8

In a bowl, sift together the flour, baking powder, baking soda, and salt. In another bowl, beat together the eggs and buttermilk. Pour into the dry ingredients and mix until a smooth batter forms. Fold in the 4 Tbsp melted butter and the blueberries.

Heat a large frying pan over medium-high heat until hot. Brush with melted butter. For each pancake, ladle 2 Tbsp of the batter into the pan, forming circles 4–5 inches (10–13 cm) in diameter. Cook until bubbles form on the surface, about 3 minutes. Turn the pancakes and cook until lightly browned on the second sides, about 3 minutes. Transfer to a platter. Repeat until all the batter is used, brushing the pan with more butter as needed. Serve the pancakes right away.

serve with

Accompany these featherlight pancakes with the classic pairing of butter and maple syrup or opt for more fruit: top with nectarine or peach slices, a dollop of sour cream, and a sprinkle of brown sugar.

winter warmer

In winter, replace the blueberries with diced ripe pears and serve with porcelain mugs of hot mint tea sweetened with a spoonful of local honey.

Brioche is truly the Queen of Breads: rich and velvety with buttery undertones that will instantly melt every shred of resistance.

brioche french toast with figs

2 large eggs

¾ cup (6 fl oz/180 ml) whole milk

¼ cup (2 fl oz/60 ml) fresh orange juice

1 Tbsp sugar

2 tsp grated orange zest

½ tsp pure vanilla extract

⅛ tsp salt

2 tsp unsalted butter

8 slices day-old brioche, ¾ inch (2 cm) thick, with crusts

8 fresh figs, quartered lengthwise

Pure maple syrup

serves 8

In a bowl, whisk together the eggs, milk, orange juice, sugar, orange zest, vanilla, and salt. Pour the batter into a baking dish.

In a large frying pan, melt 1 tsp of the butter over medium heat and continue to heat until it foams but does not brown.

Place 4 of the bread slices in the batter and let stand for 5 seconds. Turn and let stand for 5 seconds longer. Using tongs, lift the slices from the batter, letting any excess drip back into the dish, and transfer to the hot pan. Cook until browned, about 3 minutes. Turn and cook until browned on the second sides, about 2 minutes. Using clean tongs, transfer to a platter. Repeat with the remaining butter, batter, and bread slices.

Arrange the French toast on plates, garnish with the figs, and serve. Pass the syrup at the table.

serve with

Bring out your prettiest Provençal linens, then reinforce the summer-in-the-south-of-France sensibility by serving a log of fresh goat cheese along with rosemary crackers. Dress up flutes of pink sparkling wine with a few drops of raspberry liqueur (framboise), then drop a raspberry into each glass.

lemon-ricotta pancakes with compote

3 cups (12 oz/375 g)
blackberries and/or
raspberries

½ cup (5½ oz/170 g)
pure maple syrup

2 cups (15 oz/470 g)
whole-milk ricotta
cheese

⅓ cup (2 oz/60 g)
all-purpose flour

3 large eggs,
separated

3 Tbsp sugar

2 Tbsp unsalted
butter, melted

Grated zest of
1 lemon

1 tsp pure
vanilla extract

Canola oil for cooking

serves 4

To make the compote, in a saucepan, cook the berries and maple syrup over medium heat, stirring occasionally, just until the berries begin to release some juices, about 3 minutes. Set aside.

In a bowl, whisk together the ricotta, flour, egg yolks, sugar, melted butter, lemon zest, and vanilla. In another bowl, using an electric mixer, beat the egg whites on high speed until soft peaks form. Gently and evenly fold the egg whites into the batter.

Heat a griddle over medium heat until hot. Lightly oil the griddle. For each pancake, pour about ¼ cup (2 fl oz/60 ml) of the batter onto the griddle and cook until bubbles form on the surface, about 1½ minutes. Turn the pancakes and cook until golden on the second sides, about 1 minute. Transfer to a platter. Repeat until all of the batter is used, oiling the griddle as needed.

Serve the pancakes with the berry compote on the side.

serve with

Pairing the pancakes with a substantial centerpiece, like a Cured Fish Platter (page 101), will make a wholesome brunch menu. To encourage lingering, serve frosty silver mugs of mint julep.

easy variation

The pancakes are equally delicious served with uncooked fresh fruit, such as sliced peaches, apricots, or plums.

My lazy morning head loves a dish that requires very little attention: pancakes, without the flipping. Heaven.

nectarine-almond oven pancake

6 Tbsp (3 oz/90 g)
unsalted butter

½ cup (2½ oz/75 g)
all-purpose flour

1 Tbsp granulated
sugar

½ tsp salt

½ cup (4 fl oz/125 ml)
whole milk

3 large eggs

3 ripe nectarines
or peaches, pitted
and sliced

2 Tbsp firmly packed
light brown sugar

2 tsp fresh
lemon juice

¼ cup (1 oz/30 g)
sliced almonds,
lightly toasted

Confectioners' sugar
for serving

serves 4

Preheat the oven to 375°F (190°C). Put 4 Tbsp (2 oz/60 g) of the butter in a 10-inch (25-cm) ovenproof frying pan. Heat in the oven until the butter is melted, about 2 minutes. Pour out and reserve 2 Tbsp of the butter; leave the remaining butter in the pan.

In a bowl, whisk together the flour, granulated sugar, and salt. Make a well in the center and pour in the milk, eggs, and reserved 2 Tbsp melted butter. Whisk just until combined. Pour into the hot pan. Bake until the edges of the pancake are puffed and golden brown, about 20 minutes.

Meanwhile, in another frying pan, melt the remaining 2 Tbsp butter over medium heat. Add the nectarines, brown sugar, and lemon juice and cook, stirring occasionally, until the nectarines give off their juices and the brown sugar melts, about 3 minutes. Remove from the heat.

Remove the pan from the oven. Pour the nectarine mixture into the center of the pancake. Sprinkle with the almonds and dust lightly with confectioners' sugar. Cut into wedges and serve.

serve with

Goblets of Sparkling Ginger Lemonade (page 158) will awaken the taste-buds, and bowls of plain Greek yogurt, drizzled with honey and strewn with chopped pistachio nuts, will add cool crunch to your menu.

variation

Instead of nectarines or peaches, use any fruit that is in season, such as blueberries or blackberries in summer or apples or pears in autumn.

jam-filled sweet crepes

4 large eggs

1¾ cups (14 fl oz/
430 ml) whole milk,
or as needed

⅓ cup (2 oz/60 g)
all-purpose flour

2 Tbsp sugar

½ tsp salt

About 5 Tbsp
(2½ oz/75 g)
unsalted butter

Assorted jams, such
as blackberry, cherry,
plum, and strawberry,
for serving

serves 4–8

In a large bowl, whisk together the eggs and 1¾ cups milk. Slowly add the flour, sugar, and salt, whisking constantly to avoid lumps. Cover and refrigerate for 2 hours. When ready to cook, stir the batter well. It should be the consistency of heavy cream. If it is too thick, thin with a little more milk.

Heat a 12-inch (30-cm) frying pan with low, sloping sides over medium-high heat. Add about 1 tsp of the butter. Tilt the pan from side to side to coat the bottom with the butter as it melts. For each crepe, pour about ¼ cup (2 fl oz/60 ml) of the batter into the pan, quickly tilting and swirling the pan to coat the bottom with the batter. Pour any excess batter back into the bowl and return the pan to the heat. Cook until the center of the crepe bubbles and the edges begin to dry, about 30 seconds. Using tongs, turn the crepe and cook until golden on the second side, about 20 seconds. Transfer the crepe to a plate. Repeat with the remaining butter and batter, adding about 1 tsp butter to the pan before cooking each crepe. Stack the crepes on the plate, putting a piece of wax paper between them. You should have 16 crepes.

To serve, put the jams in small bowls. Invite guests to take 2–4 crepes, fill them with the jam(s) of choice, and fold or roll the crepes over the jam.

serve with

Pull out the stops with a Ramos Fizz (page 165), and provide protein for the rest of the day with Chicken-Apple Sausages (page 144). Complement the sticky-sweet jams with some tart fresh berries to awaken the sleepy palate.

Who doesn't love crepes? They are sublime, deeply satisfying, and both exotic and comforting. They are also ideal to serve for brunch, light and airy and equally suited for sweet or savory fillings.

cheese blintzes with cherry compote

for the cherry compote

½ cup (4 oz/125 g) sugar

1 cup (6 oz/185 g) pitted sweet cherries

2 tsp fresh lemon juice

¼ tsp almond extract

for the batter

1 cup (5 oz/155 g) all-purpose flour

½ tsp salt

3 large eggs

¾ cup (6 fl oz/180 ml) whole milk

3 Tbsp unsalted butter, melted, plus more for cooking

for the filling

1 cup (8 oz/250 g) farmer cheese

1 cup (8 oz/250 g) whole-milk ricotta cheese

2 Tbsp sugar

¼ tsp grated orange zest

½ tsp pure vanilla extract

4 Tbsp (2 oz/60 g) unsalted butter

serves 6

To make the cherry compote, in a small saucepan, combine the sugar and ½ cup (4 fl oz/125 ml) water. Bring to a simmer over low heat, stirring until the sugar dissolves. Add the cherries and cook just until warmed through, about 5 minutes. Transfer to a bowl and stir in the lemon juice and almond extract. Let cool to room temperature. (The compote can be made 3 days ahead and stored in the refrigerator; bring to room temperature before serving.)

To make the batter, in a bowl, whisk together the flour and salt. Add the eggs, the milk, and ¾ cup (6 fl oz/180 ml) water and whisk until smooth. Whisk in the 3 Tbsp melted butter. Cover and refrigerate for 1 hour. Alternatively, combine the eggs, milk, and water in a food processor and process until smooth, about 4 seconds; add the melted butter and process to mix. Pour into a bowl, cover, and refrigerate for 20 minutes.

Heat a large frying pan over medium heat until hot. Brush with about ½ tsp butter, then ladle ¼ cup (2 fl oz/60 ml) batter onto the center. Tilt the pan to cover the bottom evenly. Cook until the edges begin to brown and the top is set, 1½–2 minutes. Turn and cook for about 1 minute. Transfer to a plate. Repeat to make about 12 blintzes total, buttering the pan as needed and stacking the finished blintzes with waxed paper between them.

To make the filling, in a bowl, stir together the cheeses, sugar, orange zest, and vanilla until well blended.

Spread a generous 2½ Tbsp of the filling on the center of each blintz. Fold in the sides and then the ends to enclose the filling and form a rectangle. In a large frying pan, melt 2 Tbsp of the butter over medium heat. Add half of the blintzes, seam side down, and fry until lightly browned, about 2 minutes. Gently turn and fry until lightly browned on the second sides, about 2 minutes. Transfer to a plate. Repeat with the remaining blintzes and butter. Serve hot with the compote.

serve with

Serve your appreciative guests rashers of crisp bacon slices, and pour freshly squeezed orange juice to echo the orange zest–perfumed cheese filling. Round out the menu with Baked Eggs with Spinach and Cream (page 79).

gingerbread-spiced apple pancakes

1 cup (8 fl oz/250 ml) apple juice

1 cup (11 oz/345 g) pure maple syrup

2 Golden Delicious or Granny Smith apples, peeled and cored

2¼ cups (11½ oz/ 360 g) all-purpose flour

¼ cup (2 oz/60 g) firmly packed light brown sugar

2 tsp baking powder

¼ tsp baking soda

½ tsp ground cinnamon

½ tsp ground allspice

½ tsp ground ginger

¼ tsp freshly grated nutmeg

½ tsp salt

1¾ cups (14 fl oz/ 430 ml) whole milk, or as needed

2 large eggs

2 Tbsp unsalted butter, melted, plus more for serving

Canola oil for cooking

serves 4

In a small saucepan, bring the apple juice to a boil over high heat. Continue to boil until reduced to about ⅓ cup (3 fl oz/80 ml), about 10 minutes. Remove from the heat and whisk in the maple syrup. Cover and set aside.

Using a food processor fitted with the shredding disk or the large holes of a box grater-shredder, shred the apples. You should have about 1½ cups (6 oz/185 g). In a large bowl, sift together the flour, brown sugar, baking powder, baking soda, cinnamon, allspice, ginger, nutmeg, and salt. In a bowl, whisk together the 1¾ cups milk, eggs, and 2 Tbsp melted butter. Pour over the flour mixture and add the shredded apples. Stir just until combined. Do not overmix.

Heat a griddle over high heat until hot. Lightly oil the griddle. For each pancake, pour about ⅓ cup (3 fl oz/80 ml) of the batter onto the griddle and spread it slightly with the back of the measuring cup. Be careful not to crowd the pan. Cook until bubbles form and break on the surface, about 1½ minutes. Turn the pancakes and cook until golden brown on the second sides, about 1 minute. Transfer to a platter. Repeat until all the batter is used, oiling the griddle as needed. If the batter begins to thicken, thin it with a bit more milk. Serve the pancakes with butter, and pass the apple-maple syrup at the table.

serve with

Add color and crunch to the menu with Baby Spinach Salad with Roasted Strawberries (page 114), and serve sausages for a protein-rich side. Fresh-brewed coffee will soothe anyone still shaking off the mantle of sleep. Serve it in mugs, glasses, or bone-china cups with a pretty sugar and creamer set, a welcome sight for those who would rather stay in bed.

vanilla bean belgian waffles with berries and whipped cream

1½ cups (12 fl oz/ 375 ml) whole milk

1 vanilla bean, split lengthwise

2 pt (1 lb/500 g) blueberries or strawberries

7 Tbsp (3½ oz/105 g) granulated sugar

Canola oil for cooking

3 large eggs, separated

½ cup (4 oz/ 125 g) unsalted butter, melted

1¾ cups (9 oz/280 g) all-purpose flour

2 tsp baking powder

¼ tsp salt

Whipped cream (page 17) for serving

Confectioners' sugar for serving

serves 6–8

In a small saucepan, heat the milk over medium heat until bubbles form around the edges. Remove from the heat. Using the tip of a small knife, scrape the vanilla seeds into the pan. Add the pod and let stand for 30–60 minutes.

If using strawberries, slice them. In a bowl, toss the berries with 4 Tbsp (2 oz/60 g) of the granulated sugar. Macerate, stirring occasionally, until the berries soften and form a syrup, 30–60 minutes. Using a paper towel, lightly oil the grid of a Belgian waffle iron with canola oil, then preheat the iron.

In a bowl, using an electric mixer, whip the egg whites on medium-high speed until soft peaks form, about 3 minutes. Add the remaining 3 Tbsp sugar and whip until firm peaks form, 2–3 minutes. Remove the vanilla pod from the milk and pour the infused milk into a bowl. Slowly whisk in the egg yolks and butter.

In a large bowl, stir together the flour, baking powder, and salt. Make a well in the center and pour in the milk mixture, stirring until just combined. Gently fold in the egg whites.

Following the manufacturer's instructions, ladle some of the batter onto the grid of the waffle iron, close the lid, and cook until the waffle is golden brown and crisp and steam is no longer escaping from the sides of the iron. The timing will depend on the iron.

Transfer the waffle to a plate and serve right away, or place on a baking sheet in a 200°F (95°C) oven for up to 20 minutes before serving. Repeat with the remaining batter, being careful not to stack the waffles on the sheet. Top with the berries and whipped cream, and dust with confectioners' sugar.

serve with

A good brunch always includes both sweet and savory dishes, and many people like to start their day with protein. Acorn Squash and Chorizo Tart (page 105) makes an excellent pairing here. For something decadent, serve hot chocolate dusted with cinnamon and, if desired, spiked with Kahlúa or Tia Maria.

Waffles have intriguing little nooks and crannies that welcome rich toppings and an unrestrained hand with garnishing. Take a bite. Wipe chin. Repeat.

blackberry coffee cake

2 cups (10 oz/315 g)
all-purpose flour,
plus 1 Tbsp

½ tsp baking powder

½ tsp baking soda

½ tsp salt

1 cup (8 oz/250 g)
unsalted butter

1¾ cups (14 oz/440 g)
granulated sugar

Grated zest of 1 orange

2 large eggs

1 tsp pure
vanilla extract

1 cup (8 oz/250 g)
sour cream

1 pt (8 oz/250 g)
blackberries

2 Tbsp firmly packed
light brown sugar

1 tsp ground cinnamon

for the pecan streusel

¾ cup (4 oz/125 g)
all-purpose flour

⅓ cup (2½ oz/75 g)
firmly packed light
brown sugar

6 Tbsp (3 oz/90 g)
unsalted butter, at
room temperature

1 cup (4 oz/125 g)
coarsely chopped
pecans

serves 12

Preheat the oven to 350°F (180°C). Lightly butter a 9-by-13-inch (23-by-33-cm) baking dish. Dust the dish with flour, tapping out the excess.

In a bowl, sift together the 2 cups flour, baking powder, baking soda, and salt. In another bowl, using an electric mixer, beat the butter, granulated sugar, and orange zest on high speed until light in color and texture, about 3 minutes. Gradually beat in the eggs, and then the vanilla. Reduce the speed to low and add the dry ingredients in 3 additions alternately with the sour cream in 2 additions, beginning and ending with the dry ingredients and beating until smooth after each addition.

In a small bowl, gently stir together the blackberries, brown sugar, cinnamon, and the 1 Tbsp flour. Spread half of the batter in the prepared dish. Top with the berry mixture, taking care that the berries do not touch the sides of the dish. Spread the remaining batter over the berries, smoothing the top.

To make the streusel, in a small bowl, stir together the flour, brown sugar, and butter. Using your fingers, work the ingredients together just until combined. Work in the pecans. Press into a ball, and then separate with your fingers into coarse crumbs. Sprinkle the streusel evenly over the batter.

Bake until a toothpick inserted into the center of the cake comes out clean, about 45 minutes. Let cool in the dish on a wire rack for 15 minutes. Cut the cake into squares and serve.

serve with

Crescents of chilled melon provide a welcome beginning at breakfast. Add a substantial main course, like Polenta with Poached Eggs, Prosciutto, and Pecorino (page 87), to round out the menu.

special touch

Hot coffee becomes irresistible when dressed up with good brandy and dollops of thick, rich softly whipped cream.

Succulent berries stud these puffy golden confections like rubies on a beautiful brooch. Each bite of these muffins carries a wonderful burst of berry flavor.

raspberry-lemon muffins

2 cups (10 oz/315 g) all-purpose flour

1½ tsp baking powder

½ tsp ground cinnamon

½ tsp salt

2 large eggs

1 cup (8 fl oz/250 ml) whole milk

⅔ cup (5 fl oz/160 ml) canola oil

1⅓ cups (9½ oz/ 295 g) firmly packed light brown sugar

2 tsp grated lemon zest

2 Tbsp fresh lemon juice

1 tsp pure vanilla extract

¼ tsp almond extract

1 cup (4 oz/125 g) fresh or frozen raspberries

serves 6

Preheat the oven to 375°F (190°C). Line 12 standard muffin cups with paper liners or grease with butter.

In a bowl, stir together the flour, baking powder, cinnamon, and salt. In a large bowl, whisk together the eggs and milk until blended. Add the oil, brown sugar, lemon zest and juice, vanilla, and almond extract and whisk just until blended. Add the dry ingredients and stir with a rubber spatula just until moistened. Do not overmix. Fold in the berries.

Spoon the batter into the prepared muffin cups, filling each to within ¼ inch (6 mm) of the rim. Bake until a toothpick inserted into the center of a muffin comes out clean, 15–20 minutes if using fresh raspberries or about 25 minutes if using frozen raspberries. Let the muffins cool in the pan on a wire rack for 15 minutes, then unmold onto the rack. Serve warm or at room temperature.

serve with

Brighten the morning with a refreshing Stone Fruit Salad with Lime-Mint Sugar (page 111), then offer a simple herb-flecked omelet or Mushroom Omelet with Parmesan and Thyme (page 71).

maple-coconut granola
with yogurt and mango

for the granola

3 cups (9 oz/280 g)
old-fashioned
rolled oats

2 cups (10 oz/315 g)
coarsely chopped
almonds, pecans,
or walnuts

1 cup (4 oz/125 g)
shredded dried
coconut

1 cup (4 oz/125 g)
raw sunflower seeds

½ cup (3½ oz/105 g)
firmly packed light
brown sugar

½ cup (5½ oz/170 g)
pure maple syrup

⅓ cup (3 fl oz/80 ml)
canola oil

1 tsp ground cinnamon

1½ cups (9 oz/280 g)
raisins

for each serving

about ½ cup
(2½ oz/75 g) Maple-
Coconut Granola

about ⅓ cup
(4 oz/125 g) plain
Greek yogurt

about ½ cup (3 oz/
90 g) peeled, pitted,
and diced mango

Honey for drizzling

serves 20

Preheat the oven to 300°F (150°C). Lightly oil a deep roasting pan.

Place the oats, almonds, coconut, and sunflower seeds in the prepared pan and mix well. In a bowl, whisk together the brown sugar, maple syrup, oil, and cinnamon until the sugar dissolves. Pour over the oat mixture and mix well with your hands until the mixture is thoroughly moistened.

Bake, stirring every 10 minutes and being sure to move the granola from the edges of the pan into the center, until it is noticeably crispier, 45–55 minutes. Let cool completely in the pan. Stir in the raisins. (The granola can be stored at room temperature in an airtight container for up to 1 month.)

For each serving, combine the granola, yogurt, and mango in a bowl, or layer in a large parfait glass. Drizzle with honey and serve.

serve with

Start the meal with tumblers of Honey-Tangerine Fizz (page 159), then continue with the bright and healthy crunch of granola. Those with bigger appetites will appreciate a platter of Dungeness crab cakes (page 102), which keep the menu light and flavorful.

steel-cut oats with honeyed pears and glazed pecans

¼ tsp salt

1 cup (6 oz/185 g) steel-cut oats

1 tsp unsalted butter, plus 1 Tbsp

½ cup (2 oz/60 g) pecans

2 tsp sugar

2 ripe, juicy pears, such as Comice or Anjou, peeled, cored, and cut into chunks

3 Tbsp honey

¼ tsp ground cinnamon

Half-and-half, heavy cream, or whole milk for serving

serves 4

In a heavy saucepan, bring 4 cups (32 fl oz/1 l) water and the salt to a boil over high heat. Stir in the oats and return to a boil. Reduce the heat to medium-low and simmer uncovered, stirring frequently to avoid scorching, until the oats are done to your preferred texture, 25–35 minutes.

In a frying pan, melt the 1 tsp butter over medium heat. Add the pecans and sprinkle with the sugar. Cook, stirring constantly, until the sugar melts and the pecans are toasted and glazed, about 1 minute. Transfer to a chopping board. Let the pecans cool slightly, then coarsely chop. Rinse out the frying pan.

Just before the oatmeal is done, melt the 1 Tbsp butter over medium heat in the same pan. Add the pears and cook, stirring occasionally, until they give off some juices and are heated through, about 3 minutes. Add the honey and cinnamon and stir just until the honey melts.

Spoon the oats into bowls. Top with the pears and their juices and the pecans. Drizzle with half-and-half and serve.

serve with

Follow these bowls of steaming oatmeal with fried eggs (page 65), Chicken-Apple Sausages (page 144), and a few slices of your favorite toast. Pour big mugs of dark-roast coffee to accompany this hearty cool-weather brunch.

variation

Substitute Golden Delicious apples for the pears. Add a sprinkling of minced crystallized ginger to the topping.

I used to think of oatmeal as old-fashioned, even stodgy. No more. Now I serve it all the time, with various toppings or with slivers of the best butter I can find.

coffee cake muffins

for the streusel

¼ cup (1½ oz/45 g) all-purpose flour

¼ cup (2 oz/60 g) firmly packed light brown sugar

3 Tbsp cold unsalted butter, cut into chunks

2 cups (10oz/315 g) all-purpose flour

2 tsp baking powder

½ tsp baking soda

¼ tsp salt

½ cup (4 oz/125 g) cold unsalted butter, cut into chunks

½ cup (4 oz/125 g) granulated sugar

2 large eggs

2 tsp pure vanilla extract

1 cup (8 oz/250 g) sour cream

¼ cup (2½ oz/75 g) preserves, such as peach, apricot, or blackberry

serves 6–8

Preheat the oven to 400°F (200°C). Line 12 standard muffin cups with paper liners or grease with butter.

To make the streusel, in a small bowl, stir together the flour and brown sugar. Scatter the butter over the top and work in with your fingers until the mixture forms small pieces. Cover and freeze while you make the batter.

In a bowl, sift together the flour, baking powder, baking soda, and salt. In the bowl of a stand mixer fitted with the paddle attachment, beat the butter and granulated sugar on medium-high speed until fluffy, about 1 minute. Beat in the eggs, one at a time, then the vanilla, until well combined. Add the sour cream and beat on low speed to combine. Add the dry ingredients and, using a rubber spatula, stir just until evenly moistened. The batter will be quite thick.

Spoon a heaping Tbsp of the batter into each prepared muffin cup, enough to cover the bottom. Spoon 1 tsp of the preserves into the center of the batter in each cup. Top with another spoonful of batter. The cups should be full. Sprinkle each with a big pinch of the streusel.

Bake until the muffins are golden brown and a toothpick inserted into the center of a muffin comes out clean, about 15 minutes. Let the muffins cool in the pan on a wire rack for about 5 minutes, then unmold onto the rack. Serve warm.

Note: Don't let the muffins sit in the pan too long to cool or the bottoms will become soggy. Grasp the muffin pan with a hot pad to tip the muffins onto a wire rack and use a paring knife to help coax any stubborn muffins from the pan.

serve with

There's a special surprise inside these crispy streusel-topped muffins: a mouthful of sweet fruit preserves. Add to the fruit theme by serving Nectarines with Arugula and Burrata (page 117). Once the muffins are fresh out of the oven and the nectarines, arugula, and cheese are assembled, you will be free to fry or scramble eggs (pages 64–65) to order.

Ginger is such a happy-go-lucky flavor. It makes me want to jump right out of bed and head for the brunch table.

ginger-apricot muffins

2¼ cups (11½ oz/ 360 g) all-purpose flour

1 cup (8 oz/250 g) granulated sugar

1 Tbsp baking powder

¼ tsp salt

⅔ cup (5 fl oz/160 ml) canola oil

½ cup (4 fl oz/125 ml) whole milk

2 large eggs

⅓ cup (3 fl oz/80 ml) apricot nectar

½ cup (3 oz/90 g) finely chopped crystallized ginger

¼–½ cup (2½–5 oz/ 75–155 g) apricot preserves

2 Tbsp coarse sugar, such as turbinado

serves 6

Preheat the oven to 400°F (200°C). Line 12 standard muffin cups with paper liners, or grease with butter and dust with flour, tapping out the excess. Butter the top of the muffin pan.

In a bowl, sift together the flour, granulated sugar, baking powder, and salt. In another bowl, whisk together the oil, milk, eggs, and apricot nectar. Pour the milk mixture over the dry ingredients and stir together just until combined. Fold in the crystallized ginger.

Spoon half of the batter evenly among the prepared cups. Spoon 1–2 tsp of the apricot preserves into each cup, taking care that the preserves do not touch the side of the cup. Top with the remaining batter, covering the preserves. Sprinkle with the coarse sugar.

Bake until the muffins are golden brown and a toothpick inserted into the center of a muffin comes out clean, about 20 minutes. Let cool in the pan on a wire rack for 15 minutes, then unmold onto the rack and let cool slightly before serving.

Note: To make glazed muffins, omit the coarse sugar. While the muffins are baking, in a small saucepan, stir together 2 Tbsp apricot preserves and 1 Tbsp water or apricot liqueur. Bring to a boil over medium-low heat, stirring frequently. Simmer until slightly thickened, about 1 minute. Using a spatula, spread the preserves over the top of each baked muffin. Let cool for 5 minutes before serving.

serve with

Ginger pairs well with many flavors, so it's easy to pick dishes to serve with these muffins. Try Meyer Lemon–Crab Salad with Mango (page 126), and offer glasses of Lemon Verbena and Mint Tisane (page 168).

easy variation

Any soft fruit preserve will work well in these muffins; choose from peach, plum, berry, or even cherry.

mini ricotta doughnuts with caramel and chocolate sauces

for the chocolate sauce

4 oz (125 g) dark chocolate, coarsely chopped

½ cup (4 fl oz/125 ml) heavy cream

for the caramel sauce

1 cup (8 oz/250 g) granulated sugar

2 Tbsp unsalted butter

½ cup (4 fl oz/125 ml) heavy cream

for the doughnuts

Canola oil for deep-frying

¾ cup (4 oz/125 g) all-purpose flour

2 tsp baking powder

1 tsp grated lemon zest

¼ tsp salt

1 cup (8 oz/250 g) whole-milk ricotta

2 eggs

2 Tbsp granulated sugar

1½ tsp pure vanilla extract

Confectioners' sugar for dusting

serves 6–8

To make the chocolate sauce, place the chocolate in the top of a double boiler over (but not touching) barely simmering water and heat, stirring often, until melted. Remove from the heat. In a small saucepan, heat the cream over medium heat until very hot but not quite simmering. Whisk the hot cream into the melted chocolate until smooth. Warm gently in the top of the double boiler before using.

To make the caramel sauce, place the sugar in a heavy saucepan and add ¼ cup (25 fl oz/60 ml) water. Cook over medium-high heat, swirling the pan occasionally so that the mixture cooks evenly, until it starts to bubble and the edges begin to turn amber, 7–10 minutes. Continue cooking until the mixture turns deep amber, 3–5 minutes. Remove from the heat and very carefully add the butter (it may spatter). Carefully add the cream and swirl the pan until the caramel sauce is evenly mixed. Warm gently in the top of a double boiler before using.

To make the doughnuts, line a baking sheet with paper towels. Pour oil to a depth of 1½ inches (4 cm) into a large, heavy saucepan. Heat until the oil registers 370°F (190°C) on a deep-frying thermometer.

In a bowl, whisk together the flour, baking powder, lemon zest, and salt. In a large bowl, whisk together the ricotta, eggs, granulated sugar, and vanilla. Add the dry ingredients and whisk until well blended.

Working in batches, gently drop level tablespoonfuls of the batter into the hot oil and fry, turning occasionally, until golden, about 3 minutes. Using a slotted spoon, transfer the doughnuts to the paper towels to drain. Allow the oil to return to 370°F between batches. Dust with confectioners' sugar and serve with the sauces for dipping.

serve with

The richness of these doughnuts demands a lighter savory partner. Welcome guests with a big glass jug of Summer Fruit Rosé Sangria (page 165), then take the edge off their hunger with Avocado, Bacon and Tomato Tartines (page 92). They'll still have plenty of room for these naughty-but-nice doughnuts.

more for later

If you have leftover chocolate or caramel sauce, drizzle it on pancakes, waffles, or French toast.

There is no reason to consign something as good as polenta to dinnertime. In fact, it is perfect morning fare, both comfort food and a great energy booster.

breakfast polenta with maple syrup and blackberries

1½ tsp salt

1 cup (5 oz/155 g) coarse-ground polenta

1 cup (8 fl oz/250 ml) whole milk

⅔ cup (5½ fl oz/ 170 ml) pure maple syrup

½ cup (4 oz/125 g) mascarpone

1 cup (4 oz/125 g) blackberries

½ cup (2 oz/60 g) chopped pecans or almonds (optional)

serves 4

In a large, heavy saucepan, bring 3 cups (24 fl oz/750 ml) water and the salt to a boil. In a small bowl, stir together the polenta and milk. Gradually stir into the boiling water. Stirring constantly, bring the mixture to a boil, about 2 minutes. Reduce the heat to medium-low and cook, stirring often, until the polenta is thick and creamy, about 25 minutes. Add up to ½ cup (4 fl oz/125 ml) water, 1 Tbsp at a time, if the polenta begins to stick. (Be careful, as the hot polenta can bubble and spatter.)

Just before the polenta is ready, in a small saucepan, warm the maple syrup over low heat. Keep warm.

Spoon the polenta into bowls. Drizzle with the warm maple syrup and garnish with the mascarpone. Top with the blackberries and the nuts, if using, and serve.

serve with

Stimulate slow-moving palates with chilled flutes of Blood Orange Mimosas (page 163). Cornmeal loves pork, so treat guests to a big platter overflowing with crispy thick-sliced bacon. Emphasize the sunny yellow hue of polenta with rich yellow linens and a rustic tub of sunflowers.

orange marmalade bread and butter pudding

1 loaf (1 lb/500 g) challah or brioche, ends trimmed, cut into 12 slices

3 Tbsp unsalted butter, at room temperature

3 large eggs

5 large egg yolks

1¾ cups (14 fl oz/ 430 ml) whole milk

1 cup (8 fl oz/250 ml) heavy cream

⅓ cup (3 oz/90 g) sugar

½ tsp salt

1 tsp pure vanilla extract

Pinch of ground cinnamon

Pinch of freshly grated nutmeg

½ cup (5 oz/155 g) orange marmalade

Whipped cream (page 17) for serving

serves 8

Preheat the oven to 325°F (165°C). Generously butter a 12-inch (33-cm) round or 9-by-13-inch (23-by-33-cm) baking dish.

Spread the challah slices thickly and evenly with the butter. Cut the slices in half crosswise. Lay the slices in the dish so that they overlap slightly.

In a bowl, whisk together the whole eggs, egg yolks, milk, cream, sugar, salt, vanilla, cinnamon, and nutmeg. Pour evenly over the bread. Let stand for about 30 minutes so that the bread soaks up the egg mixture, occasionally pressing down on the slices with a spatula.

Bake the pudding for 30 minutes. Meanwhile, gently warm the marmalade in a small saucepan over medium-low heat. Remove the pudding from the oven and carefully spread the marmalade over the top. Continue to bake until the top is crisp, brown, and sticky, about 10 minutes. Let stand for about 10 minutes. Serve garnished with whipped cream.

serve with

Start your guests off with a Grapefruit-Prosecco Sparkler (page 162), then follow with Warm Escarole, Egg, and Bacon Salad (page 122) served family-style on a big platter. Just when they think the menu is complete, bring out this delectable treat to steal the show.

variation

You can also use any other good-quality, somewhat-dense white or spiced bread such as cinnamon raisin bread.

You'll win over anyone with this luxurious dish, the perfect centerpiece for a cool-weather brunch. Serve with fresh grapefruit and cups of hot tea.

These cranberry-studded, crumbly, tender scones are the ideal palette for rich, lightly salted European butter.

fresh cranberry scones

1½ cups (7½ oz/ 235 g) all-purpose flour

1½ Tbsp sugar

½ tsp baking powder

¼ tsp salt

7 Tbsp (3½ oz/105 g) chilled unsalted butter, cut into small pieces

1 cup (4 oz/125 g) cranberries

1 egg

2 Tbsp fresh orange juice

serves 6

Preheat the oven to 400°F (200°C).

In a bowl, whisk together the flour, sugar, baking powder, and salt. Cut in the butter with a pastry blender or 2 knives until the mixture resembles rolled oats. Stir in the cranberries. Using a fork, mix in the egg and orange juice until a soft dough forms.

On a floured work surface, roll out the dough into a round ½ inch (12 mm) thick. Using a 2-inch (5-cm) round cookie cutter, cut out as many rounds as possible. Gather the dough scraps, roll out again, and cut more rounds. Arrange on an ungreased baking sheet.

Bake until the scones are lightly golden, about 15 minutes. Watch carefully so that the bottoms do not burn. Transfer to a wire rack and let cool for 2–3 minutes. Serve warm.

serve with

For an autumnal brunch, pair these scones with Turkey and Yukon Gold Hash (page 138). Serve with bowls of tangy, thick Greek yogurt, dusted with a little cinnamon. Offer honey on the side for drizzling.

walnut–chocolate chip banana bread

3 very ripe bananas, peeled

2 cups (10 oz/315 g) all-purpose flour

1 tsp baking soda

¼ tsp salt

6 Tbsp (3 oz/90 g) unsalted butter, at room temperature

¾ cup (6 oz/185 g) sugar

2 large eggs

½ cup (4 oz/125 g) sour cream

1 cup (6 oz/185 g) semisweet chocolate chips

1 cup (4 oz/125 g) coarsely chopped walnuts, toasted

serves 8–10

Preheat the oven to 350°F (180°C). Lightly butter a 9-by-5-inch (23-by-13-cm) loaf pan. Line the bottom and long sides of the pan with parchment paper. Butter the parchment. Dust the pan with flour, tapping out the excess.

Using a fork, mash the bananas in a small bowl; you should have about 1 cup (8 oz/250 g). In a bowl, sift together the flour, baking soda, and salt. In another bowl, using an electric mixer, beat the butter and sugar on high speed until light in color and texture, about 3 minutes. Gradually beat in the eggs and then the mashed bananas. Reduce the speed to low and add the dry ingredients in 3 additions alternately with the sour cream in 2 additions, beginning and ending with the dry ingredients and beating until smooth. Fold in the chocolate chips and half of the walnuts. Pour the batter into the prepared pan and smooth the top. Sprinkle with the remaining walnuts.

Bake until a toothpick inserted into the center comes out clean, about 1 hour. Let the bread cool in the pan on a wire rack for 5 minutes. Unmold onto the rack and remove the paper. Invert and let cool completely. Serve at room temperature.

serve with

Pour guests glasses of a crisp white wine to accompany a Mushroom Omelet with Parmesan and Thyme (page 71) and a platter of sliced tomatoes, then cap off the meal with this homey banana bread.

dark chocolate tea bread

2 cups (10 oz/315 g) all-purpose flour

½ cup (2 oz/60 g) cake flour

¾ cup (2 oz/60 g) unsweetened Dutch-process cocoa powder

1 tsp baking soda

1 tsp baking powder

½ tsp salt

5 Tbsp (2½ oz/75 g) unsalted butter, at room temperature

¼ lb (125 g) cream cheese, at room temperature

1 cup (8 oz/250 g) granulated sugar

2 large eggs

1¼ cups (10 fl oz/ 310 ml) buttermilk

1½ tsp pure vanilla extract

⅔ cup (3½ oz/105 g) chopped toasted hazelnuts

1 Tbsp coarse sugar, such as turbinado

serves 8–10

Preheat the oven to 350°F (180°C). Butter a 9-by-5-inch (23-by-13-cm) loaf pan.

In a bowl, stir together the all-purpose flour, cake flour, cocoa, baking soda, baking powder, and salt. In another bowl, using an electric mixer, beat the butter and cream cheese on medium speed until fluffy. Beat in the granulated sugar until combined. Add the eggs, one at a time, beating well after each addition. The mixture should be fluffy. Add the dry ingredients in 2 additions, alternating with the buttermilk and the vanilla, beginning and ending with the dry ingredients and beating until smooth after each addition. Fold in half of the hazelnuts just until evenly distributed. The batter should be very thick.

Scrape the batter into the prepared pan. The pan should be no more than two-thirds full. Smooth the top and sprinkle with the coarse sugar and the remaining hazelnuts.

Bake until the top is firm to the touch and the edges pull away from the pan sides, about 1¼ hours. A toothpick inserted into the center should come out clean. If necessary, cover loosely with aluminum foil for the last 10 minutes to prevent overbrowning. Unmold the loaf onto a wire rack, invert, and let cool completely before serving.

serve with

Kick off your brunch menu with a Peach Bellini (page 163) and cups of hot coffee and Earl Grey tea. This refined bread deserves an elegant savory partner, such as Salade Niçoise with Seared Salmon (page 121).

cinnamon rolls with cream cheese icing

for the yeast dough

1 cup (8 fl oz/250 ml) whole milk

½ cup (4 oz/125 g) granulated sugar

5 Tbsp (2½ oz/75 g) unsalted butter, melted and cooled

3 large eggs

1 package (2½ tsp) quick-rise yeast

5 cups (25 oz/780 g) all-purpose flour

1¼ tsp salt

for the filling

½ cup (3½ oz/105 g) firmly packed light brown sugar

6 Tbsp (3 oz/90 g) unsalted butter, at room temperature

2 tsp ground cinnamon

for the icing

1½ cups (6 oz/185 g) confectioners' sugar

2 oz (60 g) cream cheese, at room temperature

2 Tbsp unsalted butter, at room temperature

½ tsp pure vanilla extract

Grated zest of 1 orange

About 4 Tbsp whole milk

serves 8

To make the dough, in the bowl of a stand mixer fitted with the paddle attachment, combine the milk, sugar, butter, eggs, and yeast. Add 4½ cups (22½ oz/705 g) of the flour and the salt. Mix on medium-low speed, adding as much of the remaining flour as needed to make a soft dough that does not stick to the bowl. Remove the paddle attachment and fit the mixer with the dough hook. Knead the dough on medium-low speed, adding more flour if needed, until the dough is smooth but still soft, 6–7 minutes. Shape the dough into a ball. Butter a large bowl. Add the dough and turn to coat with the butter. Cover tightly with plastic wrap. Let the dough rise in a warm spot until it doubles in bulk, 1½–2 hours. (Alternatively, punch down the dough, cover tightly with plastic wrap, and refrigerate for up to 12 hours. Punch down and let stand at room temperature for 1 hour before using.)

To make the filling, in a bowl, using an electric mixer on medium speed, beat together the brown sugar, butter, and cinnamon until combined, about 30 seconds.

Punch down the dough and turn out onto a floured work surface. Dust the top with flour. Roll out into a 16-by-14-inch (40-by-35-cm) rectangle, with a long side facing you. Spread the filling evenly over the dough, leaving a 1-inch (2.5-cm) border at the top and bottom. Starting at the long side of the rectangle farthest from you, roll up the rectangle into a log. Pinch the seams to seal. Cut the log crosswise into 8 equal slices.

Butter a 9-by-13-inch (23-by-33-cm) baking pan or a large, heavy ovenproof frying pan. Arrange the slices, cut side up, in the pan. Cover loosely with plastic wrap and let rise in a warm spot until doubled in bulk, 1¼–1½ hours. (Alternatively, refrigerate overnight until doubled, 8–12 hours. Remove from the refrigerator 1 hour before baking.)

Preheat the oven to 350°F (180°C). Bake until the rolls are golden brown, about 30 minutes. Let the buns cool in the pan on a wire rack for 15 minutes.

To make the icing, sift the confectioners' sugar into a bowl and add the cream cheese, butter, vanilla, and orange zest. Using an electric mixer, beat the mixture on low speed until crumbly. Gradually beat in enough of the milk to make a thick but pourable icing. Pour the icing over the warm rolls and spread using a metal icing spatula. Let cool for 15 minutes. Serve the buns warm or at room temperature.

serve with

These heavenly buns will transport most people back to a simpler time. Embrace nostalgia and serve Easy Eggs Benedict (page 89) and Spiced Iced Coffee (page 167). Today—and all its worldly cares—doesn't officially start until after you have enjoyed brunch.

variations

Sprinkle ½ cup (3 oz/90 g) raisins, dried cranberries, dried cherries, or chopped toasted pecans over the cinnamon butter before rolling up the dough.

Pungent, exotic, yet sweetly delicate, cardamom is a flavor often used in Indian dishes. Here it adds an aromatic warmth to almond-laced buns.

sweet almond buns with cardamom

¾ cup (6 fl oz/180 ml) whole milk

¼ cup (2 oz/60 g) sugar, plus 2 Tbsp

4 Tbsp (2 oz/60 g) unsalted butter, at room temperature

1 large egg

1 package (2½ tsp) quick-rise yeast

¼ tsp ground cardamom

¼ tsp almond extract

1¾ cups (9 oz/280 g) all-purpose flour

½ tsp salt

½ cup (2½ oz/75 g) finely chopped almonds

serves 12

In the bowl of a stand mixer fitted with the paddle attachment, combine the milk, ¼ cup sugar, butter, egg, yeast, cardamom, almond extract, flour, and salt and mix on low speed until a thick batter forms, about 2 minutes. Add ⅓ cup (1½ oz/45 g) of the almonds and mix just until combined.

Butter 12 standard muffin cups and dust with flour, tapping out the excess. (The batter is too sticky to use paper liners.) Divide the batter evenly among the prepared cups. Lightly oil a sheet of plastic wrap and place over the pan, oiled side down. Let stand in a warm spot until the buns have risen to the top of the pan, about 1 hour.

Preheat the oven to 350°F (180°C). In a small bowl, combine the remaining almonds and the 2 Tbsp sugar. Sprinkle evenly over the tops of the buns. Bake until the buns are golden brown, 20–25 minutes.

Let the buns cool in the pan on a wire rack for 10 minutes. Unmold and serve warm.

serve with

Start guests off with a Chai Latte (page 168), then augment the buffet table with a cool salad of Shaved Zucchini with Lemon, Mint, and Feta (page 112). For protein, cook up some rustic lamb sausages, such as *merguez*, or offer bowls of plain Greek yogurt drizzled with honey and topped with pistachio nuts.

applesauce and brown sugar crumb cake

3 cups (15 oz/470 g) all-purpose flour

1 tsp baking soda

1 tsp ground cinnamon

¼ tsp salt

1 cup (8 oz/250 g) granulated sugar

1 cup (7 oz/220 g) firmly packed light brown sugar

¾ cup (6 fl oz/ 180 ml) canola oil

¾ cup (7 oz/220 g) unsweetened applesauce

3 large eggs

3 Golden Delicious or Empire apples, peeled, cored, and cut into cubes

for the streusel

1 cup (5 oz/155 g) all-purpose flour

½ cup (4 oz/125 g) cold unsalted butter, cut into chunks

½ cup (3½ oz/105 g) firmly packed light brown sugar

serves 12

Preheat the oven to 350°F (180°C). Lightly butter a 9-by-13-inch (23-by-33-cm) baking pan. Dust the pan with flour, tapping out the excess.

In a bowl, sift together the flour, baking soda, cinnamon, and salt. In another bowl, whisk together the sugars, oil, applesauce, and eggs. Make a well in the dry ingredients and add the applesauce mixture. Stir just until smooth. Add the apples and stir until combined. Spread the batter in the prepared pan, smoothing the top.

To make the streusel, in a bowl, combine the flour, butter, and brown sugar. Using your fingers, work the ingredients together just until combined. Press together into a ball, and then separate with your fingers into coarse crumbs. Sprinkle the streusel evenly over the top of the cake.

Bake until a toothpick inserted into the center of the cake comes out clean, about 1 hour. Let the cake cool completely in the pan on a wire rack. Cut into squares and serve.

serve with

Pair Broccoli-Cheddar Quiche (page 80) with this appealingly retro crumb cake. Watercress and Grapefruit Salad (page 115), served very cold, would round out the menu nicely. Both can be made ahead, ensuring a stress-free brunch.

easy variation

Add ½ cup (2 oz/60 g) chopped toasted walnuts to the batter.

Savory

egg basics

The unassuming egg is a miracle of biological engineering: the perfect package of protein, flavor, goodness, and versatility.

scrambled eggs

12 large eggs

Kosher salt and freshly ground pepper

2 Tbsp unsalted butter

In a bowl, whisk together the eggs, ¾ teaspoon salt, and ¼ teaspoon pepper just until thoroughly blended. Do not overbeat.

In a large frying pan, preferably nonstick, melt the butter over medium-low heat until the foam begins to subside. Add the egg mixture to the pan and cook until the eggs just begin to set, about 20 seconds. Stir with a heatproof spatula, scraping up the eggs on the bottom and sides of the pan and folding them toward the center. Repeat until the eggs are barely cooked into moist curds, about 3 minutes.

Remove the pan from the heat and let the eggs stand in the pan to allow the residual heat to finish cooking them, about 1 minute. Serve at once.

serves 4–6

poached eggs

2 Tbsp distilled white vinegar

8 large eggs

Pour water to a depth of 2 inches (5 cm) into a large, deep sauté pan and add the vinegar. Bring to a gentle simmer over medium-low heat. Fill a bowl halfway with hot tap water and place it near the stove.

One at a time, crack the eggs into a ramekin or small cup and gently slide into the simmering water. Cook as many eggs as will fit comfortably in the pan and adjust the heat to keep the water at a gentle simmer. Cook until the whites are set and the yolks are glazed over but still soft, 4–5 minutes.

Using a slotted spoon, lift each egg from the water and slip it into the hot water. Just before serving, remove from the hot water with a slotted spoon, draining well and blotting the bottom of each egg briefly on paper towels. Trim any ragged edges of egg white with kitchen scissors. Serve at once.

serves 4–6

fried eggs

2 Tbsp olive oil or unsalted butter

8 large eggs

Kosher salt and freshly ground pepper

In a large frying pan, preferably nonstick, heat 1 tablespoon of the oil over medium heat. One at a time, crack 4 of the eggs into the pan. Sprinkle the eggs with salt and pepper, cover, reduce the heat to medium-low, and cook until the whites are opaque and the yolks thicken, 2–3 minutes for sunny-side-up eggs. Repeat with the remaining 1 Tbsp oil and 4 eggs. Serve at once.

To make over-easy, over-medium, or over-hard eggs, cook as directed, then, using a nonstick spatula, carefully flip the eggs and cook for about 30 seconds for eggs over easy, about 1 minute for eggs over medium, and about 1½ minutes for eggs over hard.

Note: Start with cold eggs directly from the refrigerator. The yolks are more likely to stay intact when you crack the eggs.

serves 4–6

fried eggs with asparagus, pancetta, and bread crumbs

4 slices white bread

Salt and freshly ground pepper

¼ tsp finely chopped fresh thyme or rosemary

16 asparagus spears, tough ends removed

Olive oil for drizzling

2 tsp unsalted butter, plus 2 Tbsp

2 thin slices pancetta, chopped

4 large eggs

Grated Parmesan cheese for garnish (optional)

serves 4

Cut the crusts off the bread slices and discard. Tear the bread into pieces. In a food processor, combine the bread pieces and a pinch each of salt and pepper. Process to form coarse crumbs. Add the thyme and pulse a few times, just until well mixed. You should have 1 cup (2 oz/60 g). (The crumbs can be stored in an airtight container in the freezer for up to 6 months.)

Preheat the oven to 400°F (200°C).

Spread the asparagus in a baking dish large enough to hold them in a single layer. Drizzle with the oil and season with salt and pepper. Turn the spears several times to coat them evenly. Roast the asparagus, turning once or twice, until the spears are tender-crisp and the color has darkened slightly, about 15 minutes; the timing will depend on the thickness of the spears. Remove from the oven and loosely cover with aluminum foil.

In a small frying pan, melt the 2 tsp butter over medium-high heat. Add the pancetta and sauté just until it darkens slightly, about 1 minute. Add the bread crumbs and sauté until golden, about 2 minutes. Remove from the heat.

In a large frying pan, melt the 2 Tbsp butter over medium-high heat. Break the eggs into the pan, spacing them about 1 inch (2.5 cm) apart. Reduce the heat to low and season the eggs with salt and pepper. Cover and cook until the whites are set and the yolks begin to firm around the edges, 5–7 minutes.

Just before the eggs are ready, arrange the asparagus on plates. Transfer the eggs to the plates. Sprinkle the eggs and asparagus with the bread crumb mixture. Garnish with Parmesan cheese, if using, and serve.

serve with

This is a refined menu that could easily become an afternoon repast. Create a bagel bar with smoked salmon, cream cheese, capers, slivered red onion, and minced chives. Serve with Watermelon and Shaved Celery with Feta Cheese (page 118). Pour either Peach Bellinis (page 163) or Fruit Smoothies (page 159) to complement the offerings.

zucchini, basil, and fontina quichelets

for the pastry dough

1¼ cups (6½ oz/200 g)
all-purpose flour

¼ tsp salt

7 Tbsp (3½ oz/105 g)
very cold unsalted
butter, cut into cubes

5 Tbsp (3 fl oz/
80 ml) ice water,
or as needed

2 small zucchini,
about 7 oz (220 g),
trimmed

Salt and freshly
ground pepper

3 large eggs

½ cup (4 fl oz/125 ml)
heavy cream or
half-and-half

1 Tbsp finely chopped
fresh basil

½ cup (2 oz/60 g)
shredded fontina
cheese

serves 4

To make the dough, in a food processor, stir together the flour and salt. Scatter the butter over the top and pulse for a few seconds, or just until the butter is slightly broken up into the flour but is still in visible pieces. Evenly sprinkle the ice water over the flour, then process just until the mixture starts to come together, adding more ice water, 1 tsp or so at a time, if the mixture seems too crumbly. Transfer the dough to a large resealable plastic bag and press into a flat disk. Refrigerate for 30 minutes or up to 1 day.

Preheat the oven to 400°F (200°C). Have ready four 4½-inch (11.5-cm) tartlet pans with removable bottoms.

Divide the dough into 4 equal pieces. On a floured work surface, roll each piece into a round about 6 inches (15 cm) in diameter. Line each pan with a round of dough. As you finish each one, put it in the freezer so it stays cold. Line each tart shell with aluminum foil and then fill with pie weights or dried beans. Put the shells on a baking sheet and bake until the dough is set and starting to dry out, about 15 minutes. Remove the foil and weights and continue to bake until the crusts look dry, about 5 minutes. Remove from the oven. Reduce the oven temperature to 375°F (190°C).

Meanwhile, shred the zucchini on the large holes of a box grater-shredder onto paper towels. Spread out the shreds and sprinkle with a little salt. Let stand for about 20 minutes. Using paper towels, blot the zucchini as dry as possible. Divide the shredded zucchini among the tartlet shells. In a bowl, whisk together the eggs, cream, and basil. Season with salt and pepper. Divide the mixture among the pans, pouring it over the zucchini. Sprinkle with the cheese.

Bake until the filling is set and the tops are lightly golden, about 25 minutes. If you want to get the cheese extra bubbly and brown, slide the quichelets in the broiler for 1 minute. Let stand for a few minutes before serving.

serve with

Small sausage links continue the theme of individual portions. Offer Amalfi Lemonade (page 162) for a tart and refreshing cooler. For the fruit element of this light but satisfying menu, choose ripe berries in season and let them stand, unembellished.

easy variation

You can turn this recipe into a large quiche by lining a 9-inch (23-cm) tart pan with the dough and partially baking as directed in the recipe. Add the entire amount of filling to the partially baked crust and bake as directed. It might take a few more minutes to finish baking.

mushroom omelet with parmesan and thyme

2 Tbsp unsalted
butter

¼ lb (125 g) white or
cremini mushrooms,
sliced

¾ tsp minced
fresh thyme

Salt and freshly
ground pepper

4 large eggs

2 Tbsp heavy cream

½ cup (2 oz/60 g)
shredded Parmesan
cheese

serves 2

In a frying pan, melt 1 Tbsp of the butter over medium heat. Add the mushrooms and cook, stirring occasionally, until the juices evaporate and the mushrooms begin to brown, about 6 minutes. Stir in ½ tsp of the thyme and season with salt and pepper. Transfer to a bowl.

Preheat the oven to 200°F (95°C). In a bowl, whisk together the eggs, the cream, ¼ tsp salt, and a few grinds of pepper just until blended. Do not overbeat.

Add half of the remaining 1 Tbsp butter to the pan and melt over medium heat. Tilt the pan to cover the bottom evenly with butter. Add half of the egg mixture and cook until the eggs have barely begun to set around the edges, about 30 seconds. Using a heatproof spatula, lift the cooked edges and gently push them toward the center, tilting the pan to allow the liquid egg on top to flow underneath, then cook for 30 seconds. Repeat 2 more times. When the eggs are almost completely set but still slightly moist on top, sprinkle half of the cheese over half of the omelet. Scatter half of the mushrooms over the cheese.

Using the spatula, fold the untopped half of the omelet over the filled half to create a half-moon shape. Cook the omelet for 30 seconds, then slide it onto a heatproof serving plate. Keep warm in the oven. Repeat to make a second omelet. Sprinkle the omelets with the remaining ¼ tsp thyme and serve.

serve with

For a quick and tasty wake-me-up, start with Broiled Grapefruit with Brown Sugar (page 134). Or, simply halve pink grapefruits, carefully cut out the sections for ease of eating, and scatter chopped cystallized ginger over the top. Round out the menu with Roasted Rosemary Potatoes (page 148) and small sausages.

variation

The nutty flavors of Gruyère or Comté cheese also work well with the mushrooms and can be used in place of the fontina. You can also add 1 green onion, minced, to the mushrooms during the last minute or so of cooking.

A frittata is like a painter's canvas: blank, yet rich with promise, awaiting the artist—or, in this case, the cook—and his or her whimsy.

spring vegetable frittata

16 asparagus spears, tough ends removed

Ice water

8 large eggs

2 Tbsp half-and-half

2 oz (60 g) fresh goat cheese, crumbled

½ tsp salt

½ tsp freshly ground pepper

1 Tbsp unsalted butter

1 Tbsp olive oil

2 Tbsp minced shallot

½ cup (3 oz/90 g) halved cherry tomatoes

1 Tbsp minced fresh tarragon

serves 4–6

Bring 1 inch (2.5 cm) of water to a boil in a steamer pan. Place the asparagus in the steamer rack, set over the boiling water, cover, and steam until the spears can be easily pierced with a fork, 4–5 minutes. Transfer to a bowl of ice water and let stand for 4–5 minutes to halt the cooking. Drain and cut into ½-inch (12-mm) pieces.

Preheat the broiler. In a bowl, whisk together the eggs, half-and-half, cheese, salt, and pepper until combined.

In a 14-inch (35-cm) ovenproof frying pan, melt the butter with the oil over medium heat. Add the shallot and sauté until softened, 2–3 minutes. Layer the asparagus pieces and the tomatoes in the pan, then pour the egg mixture over them. Reduce the heat to low and cook just until the eggs are set around the edges, 3–4 minutes. Using a heatproof rubber spatula, lift the edges and tip the pan so the uncooked egg runs underneath. Place the pan in the broiler 8 inches (20 cm) from the heat source and cook until the top of the frittata is set and a knife inserted into the center comes out clean, 4–5 minutes.

Remove the frittata from the broiler. Loosen the sides of the frittata with a spatula. Wearing oven mitts, invert a flat plate over the pan and, holding pan and plate together, turn them over. Lift off the pan. Sprinkle the frittata with the tarragon. Cut into wedges and serve hot, warm, or at room temperature.

serve with

Let spring be your theme for this brunch get-together: Simmer large artichokes in lemon water, then serve hot or cold with ramekins of anchovy-spiked mayonnaise. (Serve an artichoke per person or let two people share.) Roasted Rosemary Potatoes (page 148) will extend the celebration of springtime. Pair with an ice-cold dry rosé from California, France, Italy, or Spain.

roasted red pepper and potato frittata

2 red bell peppers

10 large eggs

2 Tbsp chopped fresh
cilantro, plus more
for garnish

1 Tbsp heavy cream
or whole milk

Salt and freshly
ground pepper

1 Tbsp olive oil

1 russet potato,
peeled and diced

1 yellow onion, diced

serves 4–6

Preheat the broiler. Line a baking sheet with aluminum foil. Cut each pepper in half lengthwise and remove the ribs, seeds, and stems. Place the peppers, cut side down, on the prepared sheet. Roast about 4 inches (10 cm) from the heat source, turning the peppers as needed, until blackened all over but not charred. Transfer to a heatproof bowl, cover, and let steam for 5 minutes. With wet fingers, peel away the blackened skin, then chop the peppers. Set aside.

Preheat the oven to 425°F (220°C). In a bowl, whisk together the eggs, the 2 Tbsp cilantro, the cream, and a pinch each of salt and pepper.

In a 10-inch (25-cm) ovenproof frying pan, warm the olive oil over medium heat. Add the potato and a pinch each of salt and pepper and cook, stirring occasionally, until just tender, 5–6 minutes. Add the onion and a pinch of salt and continue cooking, stirring occasionally, until the potato is golden brown and the onion is soft and translucent, 4–5 minutes. Stir in the roasted peppers and season to taste.

Reduce the heat to medium-low and pour in the egg mixture. Cook, stirring gently, until the eggs begin to set but do not start to scramble. Cook the eggs, undisturbed, until they begin to set around the edges, 2–3 minutes. Transfer the pan to the oven and bake until the eggs are set around the edges and just firm in the center, about 5 minutes.

Loosen the sides of the frittata with a spatula. Wearing oven mitts, invert a flat plate over the pan and, holding pan and plate together, turn them over. Lift off the pan. Garnish with cilantro, cut into wedges, and serve hot, warm, or at room temperature.

serve with

Begin with Cantaloupe Agua Fresca (page 163) and light Mexican beers with wedges of lime, or Micheladas (page 160). Provide protein and bright, vibrant colors with Grilled Shrimp Salad with Avocado and Chipotle Dressing (page 128).

I like to bring a frittata to the table whole, then cut it into wedges as I would a birthday cake. A pie or cake server makes quick, easy work of this task.

swiss chard, onion, and cheese frittata

1 bunch Swiss chard, about 1½ lb (750 g), tough stems removed

6 large eggs

2 Tbsp half-and-half

⅓ cup (1½ oz/45 g) shredded fontina cheese

¼ cup (1½ oz/45 g) pitted green olives, coarsely chopped

¾ tsp salt

½ tsp freshly ground pepper

2 Tbsp unsalted butter

1 Tbsp olive oil

2 Tbsp finely chopped yellow onion

1 clove garlic, minced

¼ cup (⅓ oz/10 g) chopped fresh flat-leaf parsley

1 tsp chopped fresh thyme

serves 4–6

Bring a large pot of water to a boil over high heat. Add the chard leaves, reduce the heat to medium, and cook until the leaves are tender and the ribs are easily pierced with a fork, 12–15 minutes. Drain in a sieve, rinse under cold running water, and squeeze dry. Chop finely and squeeze dry again.

In a bowl, beat together the eggs, half-and-half, cheese, olives, salt, and pepper just until blended. Stir in the chard. In a large frying pan, melt the butter with the oil over medium-high heat. Add the onion and sauté until translucent, 2–3 minutes. Add the garlic and sauté for about 1 minute. Pour in the egg mixture and reduce the heat to low. As the eggs begin to set, use a heatproof spatula to lift the edges so the uncooked egg runs underneath. Cook until the frittata is just firm around the edges and nearly set on top, 4–5 minutes.

Loosen the sides of the frittata with a spatula. Wearing oven mitts, invert a flat plate over the pan and, holding pan and plate together, turn them over. Lift off the pan, return it to the heat, and sprinkle half of the parsley and half of the thyme over the bottom. Slide the frittata, browned side up, into the pan and cook until lightly browned on the underside, 1–2 minutes. Remove from the heat and again invert the frittata onto the plate. Sprinkle with the remaining herbs, cut into wedges, and serve hot, warm, or at room temperature.

serve with

Create an artful platter of cured meats, such as salami, prosciutto, and *bresaola*. Serve with Sautéed Tomatoes with Arugula Pesto and Feta (page 141) and fresh fruit or a sweet dish of your choosing.

Creamy, fresh whole-milk mozzarella is the staff of life for me, a cheeseaholic almost since birth. Make it buffalo mozzarella to guarantee an unforgettable dish.

tomato and basil scramble with fresh mozzarella

2 tsp olive oil

1 Tbsp minced shallot

1 cup (6 oz/185 g) cherry or grape tomatoes, halved

Salt and freshly ground pepper

12 large eggs

2 Tbsp chopped fresh basil

1 Tbsp unsalted butter

¼ lb (125 g) fresh mozzarella cheese, cubed

serves 4

In a frying pan, warm the oil over medium heat. Add the shallot and cook, stirring occasionally, until softened, about 1 minute. Add the tomatoes and cook until hot and beginning to soften, about 2 minutes. Remove from the heat and season with salt and pepper. Transfer the tomato mixture to a bowl and cover with aluminum foil to keep warm.

In a bowl, whisk together the eggs, 1 Tbsp of the basil, ¾ tsp salt, and ¼ tsp pepper just until thoroughly blended. Do not overbeat.

Melt the butter in the same frying pan over medium-low heat. Add the egg mixture and cook until the eggs begin to set, about 20 seconds. Stir with a heatproof spatula, scraping up the eggs on the bottom and sides of the pan and folding them toward the center. Repeat until the eggs are barely cooked into moist curds. Add the tomato mixture and the mozzarella and stir to distribute throughout the eggs. Remove the pan from the heat and let the eggs stand in the pan to allow the residual heat to finish cooking them and melt the mozzarella, about 1 minute.

Sprinkle the remaining 1 Tbsp basil over the scramble and serve.

serve with

For a simple feast, drizzle avocado slices with fresh lemon or lime juice and garnish with finely chopped chives and minced capers; serve alongside a platter of crispy pancetta. A glass of Prosecco signals it's time to celebrate.

My first baked egg experience was a revelation: hands-off eggs loaded with nourishment and flavor but without any last-minute preparation!

baked eggs with spinach and cream

1 Tbsp unsalted butter

1½ lb (750 g) spinach, rinsed but not dried

1 tsp olive oil

3 oz (90 g) prosciutto, chopped

¾ cup (6 fl oz/180 ml) heavy cream, plus 4 tsp

Salt and freshly ground pepper

A few gratings of fresh nutmeg

4 large eggs

4 tsp grated Parmesan cheese

serves 4

Preheat the oven to 350°F (180°C). Butter four ¾-cup (6–fl oz/180-ml) ramekins.

In a large saucepan, melt the butter over medium heat. A handful at a time, add the spinach, cooking until the first batch wilts before adding another handful. Cook all of the spinach until tender, about 3 minutes. Drain the spinach in a sieve, pressing gently to remove excess liquid. Transfer to a chopping board and coarsely chop.

Heat the oil in the same saucepan over medium heat. Add the prosciutto and cook, stirring occasionally, until its fat softens, about 2 minutes. Add the spinach and the ¾ cup cream and bring to a boil. Cook, stirring often, until the cream has thickened and reduced to a few Tbsp, about 4 minutes. Season with salt, pepper, and nutmeg. Divide evenly among the prepared ramekins. Break an egg into each ramekin. Season the top of each with salt and pepper, and drizzle each with 1 tsp of the cream. Arrange the ramekins on a rimmed baking sheet.

Bake, watching the eggs carefully to avoid overcooking, until the whites are opaque and the yolks have firm edges and are soft in the center, about 15 minutes. Remove from the oven, sprinkle each serving with 1 tsp of the Parmesan, and serve.

serve with

Spike mugs of Spiced Iced Coffee (page 167) with a few dashes of applejack or Calvados, followed by Applesauce and Brown Sugar Crumb Cake (page 59). Roast some tiny red potatoes until crisp and shower with a little minced rosemary. Because a balanced morning meal typically includes fruit, assemble a dish of halved fresh apricots or plums topped with sliced almonds.

broccoli-cheddar quiche

for the pastry dough

1¼ cups (6½ oz/
200 g) all-purpose
flour

¼ tsp salt

7 Tbsp (3½ oz/105 g)
cold unsalted butter,
cut into cubes

¼ cup (2 fl oz/60 ml)
ice water, or as needed

2 cups (4 oz/125 g)
broccoli florets

1 cup (8 fl oz/250 ml)
half-and-half

2 large eggs

1 Tbsp minced
fresh dill

Salt and freshly
ground pepper

1 cup (4 oz/125 g)
shredded sharp
Cheddar cheese

serves 6

To make the dough, in a large bowl, whisk together the flour and salt. Scatter the butter over the flour. Using a pastry blender or 2 knives, cut the butter into the flour just until the mixture forms coarse crumbs about the size of peas. Drizzle the ¼ cup ice water over the mixture and toss with a fork until it forms moist clumps. If the dough seems too crumbly, add a little more ice water. Form the dough into a disk (some flakes of butter should be visible), wrap in plastic wrap, and refrigerate for at least 30 minutes or up to 2 hours. (Or, overwrap with aluminum foil and freeze for up to 1 month, then thaw in the refrigerator before using.)

Place the dough on a lightly floured work surface and dust the top with flour. (If the dough is chilled hard, let it stand at room temperature for a few minutes until it begins to soften before rolling it out.) Roll out into a round about 12 inches (30 cm) in diameter and about ⅛ inch (3 mm) thick. Transfer to a 9-inch (23-cm) tart pan with a removable bottom, gently fitting the dough into the bottom and sides of the pan. Trim the dough, leaving a ½-inch (12-mm) overhang. Fold the overhang over and into the pan, pressing it firmly against the sides; the dough should be doubly thick at the sides and rise about ⅛ inch (3 mm) above the sides of the pan rim. Pierce the dough all over with a fork. Line the dough with foil and freeze for 15–30 minutes.

Preheat the oven to 375°F (190°C). Place the dough-lined pan on a baking sheet and fill the foil with pie weights or dried beans. Bake until the dough is set and beginning to brown, about 20 minutes.

Meanwhile, bring a saucepan of lightly salted water to a boil over high heat. Add the broccoli and cook until the florets are barely tender, about 5 minutes. Drain well and pat dry. In a bowl, whisk together the half-and-half, the eggs, the dill, ½ tsp salt, and ¼ tsp pepper until combined.

Remove the baking sheet with the tart pan from the oven. Remove the foil and weights. Scatter the broccoli and cheese evenly in the pastry shell. Carefully pour the egg mixture into the shell. Return the sheet to the oven and reduce the oven temperature to 350°F (180°C). Bake until the filling is puffed and golden brown, about 35 minutes. Let cool slightly, then serve.

serve with

For a robust menu, serve with a spiral-sliced ham; add mustard whipped with fresh dill to spread on sliced baguettes before mounding with salty-sweet curls of ham. Round out this season-adaptable menu with fresh fruit. In spring, serve strawberries; in summer, switch to sliced melon or peaches, and in fall and winter serve with grapes or sliced apples and pears.

easy variation

Instead of the broccoli, use trimmed asparagus spears, cut into 1-inch (2.5-cm) lengths and blanched in boiling water until tender-crisp, about 3 minutes.

I love pulling this amazingly rich and outrageously delicious dish out of the oven right when friends arrive for brunch. It's a slam dunk.

sausage and cheddar strata

3 lb (1.5 kg) sausages, such as mild Italian, chicken and fennel, or andouille

15 slices day-old baguette, ciabatta, or other country-style bread, each about 2 inches (5 cm) in diameter and ½ inch (12 mm) thick

¼ lb (125 g) Cheddar cheese, coarsely shredded

3 large eggs

1½ cups (12 oz/ 375 ml) whole milk

serves 4–6

In a frying pan, sauté the sausages over medium heat until golden brown on all sides, 5–6 minutes for fully cooked sausages, 12–15 minutes for uncooked sausages. Transfer to a cutting board. Let the sausages cool, then cut into slices ½ inch (12 mm) thick.

Butter a deep 2½-qt (2.5-l) baking dish. Arrange one-third of the bread slices on the bottom of the prepared dish, cutting the slices if needed to fill any gaps. Top with one-third of the sausages, and then with one-third of the cheese. Repeat the layering 2 more times, ending with the cheese. In a bowl, whisk together the eggs and milk until well blended. Pour into the baking dish, being careful not to dislodge the layers. Cover and refrigerate for at least 1 hour or up to 24 hours before baking.

Preheat the oven to 350°F (180°C). Cover the dish with aluminum foil and bake for 45 minutes. Remove the foil and continue to bake until the top is golden brown and a knife inserted into the center comes out clean, about 15 minutes. Transfer the dish to a wire rack, cover loosely with foil, and let cool for about 10 minutes before serving.

serve with

Start off with lox and bagels with plenty of capers, sour cream, and slivered red onion and offer either Chai Lattes (page 168) or hot Earl Grey tea with lemon. After the strata, serve Baby Spinach Salad with Roasted Strawberries (page 114).

entertaining tip

Hot dishes—best served soon after they leave the oven— are well-suited to multicourse brunches.

cheesy egg sandwiches

6 pork sausage
patties, homemade
(page 143) or
purchased

6 slices sharp
Cheddar cheese

6 English muffins
or rolls, split

6 large eggs

Salt and freshly
ground pepper

2 Tbsp unsalted
butter

Hot-pepper sauce
for serving

serves 6

Preheat the broiler.

Heat a large frying pan over medium heat. Add the sausage patties, reduce the heat to medium-low, and cook until browned, about 5 minutes. Turn and cook until the other sides are browned and the centers feel firm when pressed with a finger, about 5 minutes. Place a slice of cheese on each patty, cover the pan, and cook until the cheese melts, about 1 minute. Transfer the patties to a paper towel–lined plate and keep warm. Discard the fat from the pan.

Place the muffin halves, cut side up, on a baking sheet and toast in the broiler until lightly crisped, about 2 minutes.

In a bowl, whisk together the eggs, ¼ tsp salt, and a few grinds of pepper just until thoroughly blended. Do not overbeat. Wipe out the frying pan with paper towels. Melt the butter over medium heat, tilting the pan to coat the bottom with the butter. Add the egg mixture and cook until the eggs have barely begun to set around the edges, about 30 seconds. Using a heatproof spatula, lift the cooked edges and gently push them toward the center, tilting the pan to allow the liquid egg on top to flow underneath, then cook for about 30 seconds. Repeat and then cover the frying pan and cook until the eggs have set into a thin omelet, about 30 seconds. Using the heatproof spatula, divide the omelet into 6 wedges.

Top 6 of the muffin halves with the sausage patties, then with the omelet wedges, folded to fit. Cover with the remaining muffin halves and serve. Pass the hot-pepper sauce at the table.

serve with

This satisfying sandwich can stand alone as a full meal, or pair with Broiled Grapefruit with Brown Sugar (page 134) and Walnut–Chocolate Chip Banana Bread (page 51). Either way, offer fresh juice and/or Micheladas (page 160).

easy variation

Of course, fried eggs (page 65) would be just as delicious as scrambled eggs. And cooked smoked ham or bacon could easily stand in for the sausage.

Picture a sunny Midwestern morning and a sleek silver Airstream trailer parked in a tree-shaded glen. I am inside, in my apron, serving up the first meal of the day.

huevos rancheros

for the ranchero sauce

1 Tbsp canola oil

1 small yellow onion, chopped

½ jalapeño chile, seeded and minced

2 cloves garlic, minced

1 can (14½ oz/455 g) diced tomatoes

½ cup (4 fl oz/125 ml) canned tomato sauce

1 tsp chili powder

1 canned chipotle pepper in adobo, chopped, plus ½ tsp adobo sauce (optional)

Salt and freshly ground pepper

4 Tbsp (2 fl oz/ 60 ml) olive oil

8 corn tortillas

8 large eggs

Salt and freshly ground pepper

½ cup (2½ oz/75 g) crumbled *queso fresco* or feta cheese

Fresh cilantro leaves for serving

Cooked black beans, warmed, for serving

serves 4

To make the ranchero sauce, in a saucepan, heat the oil over medium heat. Add the onion, chile, and garlic and cook, stirring occasionally, until softened, about 5 minutes. Transfer to a blender. Add the tomatoes and their juice, tomato sauce, chili powder, and chipotle pepper and sauce (if using) and purée. Return to the saucepan and bring to a boil over high heat. Reduce the heat to medium-low and cook, stirring frequently, until reduced to about 2 cups (16 fl oz/500 ml), about 30 minutes. Season with salt and pepper. Cover and keep warm over very low heat.

Preheat the oven to 200°F (95°C). Have ready 4 ovenproof plates large enough to hold 2 overlapping tortillas.

In a large frying pan, heat 2 Tbsp of the oil over high heat. One at a time, fry the tortillas just until they begin to crisp (they should not be crunchy), about 30 seconds. Transfer to paper towels to drain. Overlap 2 tortillas on each plate and keep warm in the oven. Discard the oil in the pan.

Add the remaining 2 Tbsp oil to the pan and heat over medium heat. Crack 4 of the eggs into the pan. Season with salt and pepper, cover, reduce the heat to medium-low, and cook until the whites are set, about 2 minutes for sunny-side-up eggs. Or carefully flip the eggs and cook to the desired doneness. Transfer 2 eggs to each of 2 plates in the oven, placing them on the tortillas, and keep warm while frying the remaining eggs.

For each serving, spoon about ½ cup (4 fl oz/125 ml) of the warm sauce over and around the eggs, top with one-fourth of the cheese, and sprinkle with cilantro. Serve hot. Pass the beans at the table.

serve with

This dish makes a filling meal all by itself, but here's how to round out the menu: Watermelon-Lime Agua Fresca (page 166) and Cinnamon Rolls with Cream Cheese Icing (page 56). Or, for a simpler accompaniment, serve Coffee Cake Muffins (page 42) or dust buttered white toast with good-quality ground cinnamon.

Andouille is a serious carnivore's dream food: a smoky, spicy, rich pork sausage that carries the true essence of the pig, Southern-style.

cajun scramble

2 tsp olive oil

½ lb (250 g) andouille or other hot smoked sausage, cubed

½ cup (2½ oz/75 g) chopped green bell pepper

½ cup (2½ oz/75 g) chopped red bell pepper

2 green onions, white and green parts, minced

1 clove garlic, minced

12 large eggs

½ tsp salt

¼ tsp hot-pepper sauce

2 Tbsp unsalted butter

½ cup (2 oz/60 g) shredded sharp Cheddar cheese

serves 4–6

In a frying pan, warm the oil over medium-high heat. Add the sausage and cook, stirring occasionally, until it begins to brown, about 5 minutes. Add the bell peppers, reduce the heat to medium, cover, and cook, stirring occasionally, until the peppers are tender, about 4 minutes. Uncover and add the green onions and garlic. Cook, stirring occasionally, until the garlic softens and is fragrant, about 2 minutes. Transfer the sausage mixture to a bowl and cover with aluminum foil to keep warm.

In a bowl, whisk together the eggs, salt, and hot-pepper sauce just until thoroughly blended. Do not overbeat.

Melt the butter in the same frying pan over medium-low heat. Add the egg mixture to the pan and cook until the eggs begin to set, about 20 seconds. Stir with a heatproof spatula, scraping up the eggs on the bottom and sides of the pan and folding them toward the center. Repeat until the eggs are barely cooked into moist curds. Add the sausage mixture and cheese and stir to distribute throughout the eggs. Remove the pan from the heat and let the eggs stand in the pan to allow the residual heat to finish cooking them and melt the cheese, about 1 minute. Serve at once.

serve with

Accompany this Cajun-inspired dish with Cheese Grits (page 151) and sliced ripe tomatoes for color and freshness. For a beverage, serve iced coffee in tall glasses or Bloody Marys topped with celery or pickled vegetables. To extend brunch into an all-day affair, set out a platter of cold poached shrimp and a pot of honey mustard for dipping.

easy variation

Substitute cubed fresh mozzarella cheese for the Cheddar.

polenta with poached eggs, prosciutto, and pecorino

2 tsp olive oil

8 thin slices prosciutto

1½ tsp salt

1 cup (5 oz/155 g) coarse-ground polenta

1 cup (8 fl oz/250 ml) whole milk

1 tsp fresh lemon juice

4 large eggs

8 Tbsp (2 oz/60 g) grated pecorino cheese

Freshly ground pepper

serves 4

In a large frying pan, warm the oil over medium heat. Add the prosciutto slices in a single layer and cook, turning once, until the slices are hot and begin to crisp at the edges, about 5 minutes. Remove from the heat and keep warm.

In a large, heavy saucepan, bring 3 cups (24 fl oz/750 ml) water and the salt to a boil over medium-high heat. In a small bowl, stir together the polenta and milk. Gradually stir the polenta mixture into the boiling water. Stirring constantly, bring the mixture to a boil, about 2 minutes. Reduce the heat to medium-low and cook, stirring frequently, until the polenta is thick and creamy, about 25 minutes. Add up to ½ cup (4 fl oz/125 ml) water, 1 Tbsp at a time, if the polenta begins to stick. (Be careful, as the hot polenta can bubble and splatter.)

Pour water to a depth of 2 inches (5 cm) into a large, deep sauté pan and add the lemon juice. Bring to a gentle simmer over medium heat. One at a time, crack the eggs into a ramekin or small cup and gently slide into the simmering water. Adjust the heat to keep the water at a gentle simmer. Cook until the whites are set and the yolks are glazed over but still soft, 4–5 minutes.

About 1 minute before the eggs are done, spoon the polenta on plates or in shallow bowls. Lay 2 prosciutto slices over each serving. Using a slotted spoon, lift each egg from the water, draining well and blotting the bottom briefly on paper towels. Trim any ragged edges of egg white with kitchen scissors. Place on the prosciutto and sprinkle each egg with 2 Tbsp of the cheese. Season lightly with salt and pepper and serve.

serve with

Start your guests off with a Balsamic Bloody Mary (page 160), and be sure to have plenty of spicy, nonalcoholic tomato juice on hand, too. This is a rich dish, so in summer, lighten the menu with Summer Vegetable Stacks (page 153). In winter, treat diners with mini ricotta doughnuts (page 45).

This is my go-to brunch dish for small gatherings. I love the way the yolks ooze into the soft, creamy polenta.

The hollandaise—rich yet ethereal—elevates this dish to iconic brunch fare. Don't skimp on the lemony, buttery sauce. If in doub double the recipe (I always do).

easy eggs benedict

for the hollandaise sauce

4 large egg yolks

2 Tbsp fresh lemon juice

Salt and freshly ground pepper

1 cup (8 oz/250 g) unsalted butter

4 English muffins, split

2 tsp white or cider vinegar

8 eggs

8 slices Canadian bacon

1–2 Tbsp butter, at room temperature

2 Tbsp chopped fresh flat-leaf parsley

serves 4

To make the hollandaise sauce, in a blender, combine the egg yolks, lemon juice, ⅛ tsp salt, and a few grinds of pepper. In a small saucepan, melt the butter over medium heat. With the blender running, slowly add the warm melted butter and process until the sauce is thick and smooth. Taste and adjust the seasoning. If the sauce is too thick, add a little water to thin it.

Transfer the hollandaise sauce to a heatproof bowl. Cover and place over (not touching) a saucepan of hot (not simmering) water to keep warm until ready to use.

Preheat the broiler and place the muffin halves on a rimmed baking sheet.

Pour water to a depth of 2 inches (5 cm) into a large, deep sauté pan and add the vinegar and a pinch of salt. Bring to a gentle simmer over medium-low heat. Fill a bowl halfway with hot tap water and set it next to the stove.

One at a time, crack the eggs into a ramekin or small cup and gently slide into the simmering water. Cook as many eggs at a time as will comfortably fit in the pan. Cook until the whites begin to set, about 2 minutes, then gently turn the eggs with a slotted spoon. Cook for another minute or so, until the whites are opaque and fully cooked and the yolks are still runny. Using the slotted spoon, lift each egg from the water, draining well. Trim any ragged edges of egg white with kitchen scissors. Transfer to the bowl of water to keep warm while you finish cooking the eggs.

Heat a frying pan over medium heat. Add the Canadian bacon and cook, turning once, until warmed through, about 2 minutes. Toast the muffin halves in the broiler until golden brown. Lightly butter the toasted muffins and place 2 halves on each plate. Top each muffin half with a slice of Canadian bacon, a warm egg, and about 2 Tbsp of the warm hollandaise sauce. Garnish with the parsley and serve.

variations

blackstone

Instead of Canadian bacon, cook 8 slices smoked bacon until crisp. Cut each bacon slice in half and place 2 pieces on each muffin half, then top with a tomato slice, the egg, and the hollandaise.

florentine

Instead of Canadian bacon, place about ¼ cup (¼ oz/7 g) firmly packed baby spinach leaves on each muffin half before adding the eggs and the hollandaise. Sprinkle with chopped fresh marjoram, about 2 tsp total, in place of the parsley.

I love watching my friends' expressions when they take that second bite of this burger and discover the hidden cheese surprise.

cheese lover's burger

3 lb (1.5 kg) ground chuck

1 Tbsp sea salt

1½ tsp freshly ground pepper

3 oz (90 g) Gorgonzola *dolce* cheese, plus more for topping

6 hamburger buns, split

suggested condiments

Butter lettuce leaves or arugula

Tomato slices

Purple onion slices, grilled or raw

Roasted red bell pepper slices

Peperoncini

serves 6

In a bowl, combine the meat, salt, and pepper and mix together with your hands. Divide the meat into 12 balls and flatten 6 of them slightly. Divide the Gorgonzola into 6 portions. In the center of each of the 6 slightly flattened balls, place a cheese portion. Place the remaining balls of meat on top and pinch the edges together. Gently flatten to make 6 patties 5–6 inches (13–15 cm) in diameter. Wrap in plastic wrap and refrigerate for at least 1 hour or up to 4 hours before cooking.

Prepare a charcoal or gas grill for direct-heat grilling over medium-high heat. Oil the grill rack.

Place the buns, cut side down, on the grill and grill until just golden, 2–3 minutes. Transfer to a plate and keep warm. Place the patties on the grill and cook for about 4 minutes per side for rare, 6–8 minutes per side for medium, and a full 10 minutes per side for well done. During the last minute of cooking, add more Gorgonzola to the top of each burger.

Serve the burgers hot with the buns and as many condiments as desired.

serve with

Start off with an ice-cold Michelada (page 160), and give the grill master's support team something fun to munch on, like a bowl of hummus with vegetable chips. In the summertime, round out the menu with Watermelon and Shaved Celery with Feta (page 118); in winter, swap in Oven-Roasted Fruit with Ricotta Cream (page 137). Arrange an array of burger toppings on a platter so guests can help themselves.

My kind of B.L.T. forgoes the second slice of bread so that I'm free to concentrate all my appetite on the best stuff. Avocado adds to the pleasure.

avocado, bacon, and tomato tartines

for the garlic aioli

4 cloves garlic, coarsely chopped

½ tsp salt

2 large eggs

2 Tbsp fresh lemon juice

1 tsp Dijon mustard

1½ cups (12 fl oz/ 375 ml) olive oil

4 slices coarse country bread, each ½ inch (12 mm) thick

2 tomatoes, cut into slices ¼ inch (6 mm) thick

Salt

8 thin slices bacon, cooked

1 avocado, halved, pitted, peeled, and thinly sliced

serves 4

To make the aioli, in a blender, process the garlic and salt. Add the eggs, lemon juice, and mustard and process again. With the motor running, slowly pour in the oil and blend until the mixture thickens to the consistency of mayonnaise. Cover and refrigerate until ready to use.

Preheat the broiler. Arrange the bread on a baking sheet. Place in the broiler and cook until lightly toasted, 2–3 minutes.

Spread the aioli on the bread and top with a few tomato slices, pressing the tomato into the bread. Season with salt. Top the tomato slices with the avocado slices, season lightly with salt, and then finish with the bacon and serve.

serve with

Give your guests the gift of a lazy afternoon of grazing. Start off with crisp radishes with butter and salt, then put out a platter of sliced mango (sprinkled with a little dark rum, if you'd like). After the savory delights, bring out Vanilla Bean Belgian Waffles with Berries and Whipped Cream (page 32).

This delightfully delicate tart adds an elegant yet unfussy note to any brunch table. Search out fresh peas in their short season, late spring into summer.

english pea and ricotta tart

8-by-10-inch (20-by-25-cm) sheet frozen puff pastry, thawed in the refrigerator

1⅓ cups (6½ oz/200 g) shelled peas

1 cup (8 oz/250 g) whole-milk ricotta cheese, drained

3 Tbsp finely chopped fresh mint, plus small leaves for garnish

1 tsp minced lemon zest

Salt and freshly ground pepper

¼ cup (¼ oz/7 g) fresh flat-leaf parsley leaves

2 green onions, white and green parts, very thinly sliced on the diagonal

Fresh lemon juice for seasoning

Pea shoots for garnish (optional)

serves 4–6

Preheat the oven to 400°F (200°C). Line a baking sheet with parchment paper. Place the puff pastry on the prepared sheet and bake until puffed, 10–13 minutes. Remove from the oven, top with a sheet of parchment paper and another baking sheet, and bake until golden and crisp, 10–13 minutes. Remove the top baking sheet and parchment paper and let cool.

Bring a pot of salted water to a boil. Add the peas and cook until tender, 2–3 minutes. Drain and rinse briefly under cold running water. Reserve ⅓ cup (1½ oz/15 g) of the peas. In a food processor, process the remaining peas, the ricotta, and 1 Tbsp of the chopped mint to make a chunky purée. Stir in the lemon zest and season with salt and pepper.

In a small bowl, combine the parsley, the remaining 2 Tbsp mint, the green onions, and the reserved peas. Season with salt and lemon juice. Spread the ricotta mixture evenly over the pastry and top with the parsley mixture. Garnish with mint leaves and with pea shoots, if desired. Cut into pieces and serve.

serve with

Start off with poached asparagus accompanied with aioli for dipping. After the tart, serve Meyer Lemon–Crab Salad with Mango (page 126). If you feel like including a little meat in the menu, you can't go wrong with crisp bacon.

spring brunch sip

Mix up a Pimm's Cup by adding sparkling lemonade or lemon-lime soda to Pimm's No. 1 in an ice-filled highball glass; add plenty of garnishes like sliced apples, orange peel, and mint.

steak and eggs

4 New York strip
steaks, about 6 oz
(185 g) each

Salt and freshly
ground pepper

2 Tbsp olive oil

½ lb (250 g) mixed
mushrooms, cut into
1-inch (2.5-cm)
pieces

½ tsp minced garlic

1 tsp minced
fresh thyme

2 Tbsp unsalted
butter

4 large eggs

serves 4

Heat a large cast-iron frying pan over medium-high heat. Generously sprinkle the steaks with salt and pepper. When the pan is hot, add 1 Tbsp of the oil and then the steaks, and cook until nicely browned, about 2 minutes. Turn and cook until browned on the second sides and medium-rare in the center, about 2 minutes. Transfer to a plate and tent with aluminum foil to keep warm.

Heat the remaining 1 Tbsp oil in the same pan over medium-high heat. Add the mushrooms, garlic, and thyme and sauté until the mushrooms are lightly browned and tender, 4–5 minutes. Season with salt and pepper and remove from the heat.

While the mushrooms are cooking, melt the butter in a large frying pan, preferably nonstick over medium heat. One at a time, crack the eggs into the pan. Season with salt and pepper, cover, reduce the heat to medium-low, and cook until the whites are opaque and the yolks thicken, 2–3 minutes for sunny-side-up eggs. If desired, using a nonstick spatula, carefully flip the eggs and cook for about 30 seconds for eggs over easy and about 1 minute for eggs over medium.

Place each steak on a plate along with a heaping spoonful of mushrooms. Top each steak with an egg and serve.

serve with

Begin with something light, like a platter of sliced fruit or a bowl of berries. Then, accompany this hearty main dish with Hash Browns (page 142) or Corn Fritters (page 148). To round out the menu and provide a sweet finish, bake a batch of Ginger-Apricot Muffins (page 43) and serve warm, with a pot of apricot jam or ginger preserves.

buckwheat crepes with smoked salmon and crème fraîche

½ cup (2½ oz/75 g) all-purpose flour

½ cup (2½ oz/75 g) buckwheat flour

½ tsp salt

2 large eggs

¾ cup (6 fl oz/180 ml) whole milk

1 Tbsp canola oil

½ lb (250 g) thinly sliced smoked salmon

1 cup (8 oz/250 g) crème fraîche

Freshly ground pepper

Finely chopped fresh chives for garnish

serves 4

In a large bowl, combine the all-purpose and buckwheat flours and the salt. Add the eggs, the milk, and ¾ cup (6 fl oz/180 ml) water and whisk until well blended. Cover and refrigerate for about 20 minutes.

Heat a 9- or 10-inch (23- or 25-cm) frying pan with low, sloping sides over medium heat. Brush lightly with some of the oil. For each crepe, pour about 6 Tbsp (3 fl oz/90 ml) of the batter into the pan, quickly tilting and swirling the pan to coat the bottom with the batter. Cook until the top of the crepe is set, about 2 minutes. Using a wide spatula, carefully turn the crepe and cook for about 1 minute. Transfer the crepe to a plate and repeat with the remaining oil and batter. Stack the crepes on the plate, putting a piece of waxed paper between them. You will have 8 crepes.

Divide the salmon evenly among the crepes, fold the crepes into quarters, and arrange on a platter. Spoon the crème fraîche on top, sprinkle with pepper and chives, and serve.

serve with

Create an inviting menu that will encourage lingering. Offer Watercress and Grapefruit Salad (page 115), adding avocado slices to the mixture. Serve poached eggs (page 64) topped with a few grains of caviar, and be sure not to skimp on freshly squeezed orange juice.

The crepe is the stylish older sister of the pancake, the one who spent her junior year studying in France and never lets you forget it.

What makes these succulent, spicy bbq shrimp so wonderfully easy is that there's no charcoal grill or barbecue sauce in sight. This recipe is a New Orleans insider's secret.

new orleans–style bbq shrimp and grits

for the grits

1⅛ cups (8 oz/250 g) stone-ground white corn grits

1⅜ cups (11 fl oz/ 330 ml) whole milk

2 tsp salt

6 Tbsp (3 oz/90 g) unsalted butter, cut into Tbsp

1½ lb (750 g) medium shrimp, peeled and deveined

1 cup (8 fl oz/250 ml) dark beer

¼ cup (2 fl oz/60 ml) Worcestershire sauce

2 Tbsp hot-pepper sauce

1 Tbsp fresh lemon juice

1 tsp minced fresh rosemary

1 Tbsp cold unsalted butter

serves 4

To make the grits, place the grits in a large bowl and add enough cold water to cover by 1 inch (2.5 cm). Let stand for 5 minutes. Skim off any bran or hulls floating on the surface. Drain the grits in a fine-mesh sieve. In a large, heavy saucepan, bring 4 cups (32 fl oz/1 l) water, the milk, and the salt to a boil over high heat. Gradually whisk in the grits. Reduce the heat to low and simmer, whisking every 5 minutes, until the grits are thick and tender, about 45 minutes. Remove from the heat and whisk in the 6 Tbsp butter, 1 Tbsp at a time.

About 10 minutes before the grits are done, heat a large frying pan over medium-high heat. Add the shrimp and cook until one side is seared, about 1 minute. Transfer to a bowl.

Add the beer, Worcestershire sauce, hot-pepper sauce, and lemon juice to the pan and stir to scrape up the browned bits on the bottom of the pan. Cook, stirring frequently, until reduced by about one-third, about 5 minutes. Return the shrimp to the pan and cook until opaque throughout, about 1 minute. Remove from the heat and stir in the rosemary. Add the butter and stir until melted and the sauce is lightly thickened (the sauce will still be thin).

Spoon the grits into bowls. Top with the shrimp and sauce, and serve.

serve with

Nobody will complain if you cook up some andouille sausages and some Brioche French Toast with Figs (page 24) to accompany these spicy shrimp. Here's a perfect opportunity to create a Bloody Mary bar where guests can create their own drinks. Provide vodka, tomato and vegetable juice, celery salt, salt, black pepper, horseradish, Worcestershire sauce, hot-pepper sauce, balsamic vinegar, lemons, and plenty of leafy celery sticks and pickled vegetables.

Cured fish is found on breakfast tables all across Northern Europe, a tradition that I enthusiastically embrace. It is a great way to put protein in the first menu of the day.

cured fish platter with accompaniments

6 slices seedless
rye bread

2 Tbsp unsalted
butter, melted

¼ lb (125 g) sliced
smoked wild salmon

¼ lb (125 g) cured
white anchovies

¼ lb (125 g) cured
sardines

¼ cup (2 oz/60 g)
capers, rinsed
and drained

½ cup (4 oz/125 g)
crème fraîche

1 lemon, cut
into wedges

serves 4–6

Preheat the oven to 350°F (180°C).

Cut each slice of bread in half on the diagonal. Arrange the halves on a baking sheet and brush with the butter. Bake until golden, 10–12 minutes. Let cool.

Arrange the salmon, anchovies, sardines, and toasted bread on a platter. Put the capers, crème fraîche, and lemon wedges in separate small bowls or on the platter with the fish. Serve, inviting guests to assemble their own combinations.

serve with

Create a sensational spread around this eye-catching platter by adding a carve-your-own ham with pumpernickel toasts and sweet mustard; your favorite granola and Greek yogurt; and Vanilla Bean Belgian Waffles with Berries and Whipped Cream (page 32).

dungeness crab cakes with cabbage slaw

for the crab cakes

½ cup (4 fl oz/125 ml) mayonnaise

2 tsp dry mustard

Salt and cayenne pepper

1 celery stalk, minced

2 green onions, minced

1 lb (500 g) cooked Dungeness crabmeat, picked over for shells

2 cups (4 oz/125 g) fresh bread crumbs

4 tsp *each* unsalted butter and canola oil

for the slaw

¼ cup (2 fl oz/60 ml) buttermilk

¼ cup (2 fl oz/60 ml) mayonnaise

2 Tbsp minced fresh dill

1 clove garlic, minced

4 cups (12 oz/375 g) thinly sliced napa cabbage

3 carrots, grated

2 green onions, white and pale green parts, minced

Salt and freshly ground black pepper

Fresh lemon juice

Lemon wedges and dill sprigs for serving

serves 4

To make the crab cakes, in a bowl, stir together the mayonnaise, mustard, and a pinch each of salt and cayenne pepper. Stir in the celery and green onions. Gently fold in the crabmeat and half of the bread crumbs. Spread the remaining bread crumbs on a sheet of waxed paper. Shape the crab mixture into 8 patties, each 1 inch (2.5 cm) thick. They will only reluctantly hold together; do not overwork them. Place each cake in the bread crumbs and turn to coat evenly. Arrange the cakes on a baking sheet, cover with plastic wrap, and refrigerate for 1 hour.

Meanwhile, to make the slaw, in a small bowl, whisk together the buttermilk, mayonnaise, dill, and garlic. In a large bowl, toss together the cabbage, carrots, and green onions. Add the dressing and toss well. Season with salt and black pepper and toss again. Add lemon juice to taste.

Heat 2 large frying pans over medium heat. In each pan, melt 2 tsp of the butter with 2 tsp of the oil. Place 4 crab cakes in each pan and cook until golden brown, about 3 minutes. Turn and cook until the cakes are well browned on the second sides and hot throughout, 3–4 minutes. Transfer to a platter or individual plates, garnish with dill sprigs, and serve with the lemon wedges and the slaw.

serve with

Accompany these savory cakes with another irresistible dish: Cinnamon Rolls with Cream Cheese Icing (page 56). Slice ripe avocados and serve with a simple drizzle of olive oil and lemon juice alongside a platter of crisp bacon.

As a kid growing up in California, I ate Dungeness crab at every opportunity. Despite that, crab still always seems special. It's a favorite centerpiece of my brunch menus.

Nearly everyone—young and old alike—likes soft-boiled eggs. They are the ultimate comfort food, garnished with just a touch of chili powder for heat.

soft-boiled eggs with rosemary-chili salt

1 tsp dried rosemary leaves

1 Tbsp salt

½ tsp chili powder

4 large eggs

serves 4

In a spice grinder or in a mortar using a pestle, grind the rosemary leaves until they are a fine powder. In a small serving bowl, combine the rosemary, salt, and chili powder and mix well with a fork. (The rosemary mixture can be stored in an airtight container at room temperature for up to 4 days.)

Place the eggs in a saucepan and add cold water to cover by 1 inch (2.5 cm). Bring to a boil over medium-high heat. When the water boils, remove the pan from the heat and cover. Let stand for 4–5 minutes for a soft egg, 6–7 minutes for a medium-soft egg, or 8 minutes for a medium egg. Using a slotted spoon, remove the eggs. Pour off the hot water and fill the pan with cold water. Return the eggs to the pan and let cool for 5 minutes.

Place each egg, pointed end down, in an egg cup and serve. Diners use a knife to crack the top half of the shell and then lift it off. Pass the rosemary-chili salt at the table.

serve with

For the sweet and protein elements on the menu, make Gingerbread-Spiced Apple Pancakes (page 31) and patties of Chicken-Apple Sausage (page 144) or Turkey and Yukon Gold Hash (page 138), along with slices of toast slathered with butter. Unfiltered apple juice or apple smoothies are a refreshing alternative to more expected juices.

acorn squash and chorizo tart

for the pastry dough

1¾ cups (9 oz/280 g) all-purpose flour

1 tsp sugar

Salt

½ cup (4 oz/125 g) cold unsalted butter, cut into small pieces

3 Tbsp solid vegetable shortening

4–5 Tbsp ice water

½ lb (250 g) acorn squash, peeled, seeded, and cut into ½-inch (12-mm) chunks

2 Tbsp olive oil

¼ lb (125 g) Spanish-style chorizo, diced

1 yellow onion, finely chopped

1 clove garlic, finely chopped

½ cup (2 oz/60 g) shredded Monterey jack cheese

1 large egg yolk

serves 6–8

Place the flour, sugar, and ½ tsp salt in a food processor and process to combine. Sprinkle in the butter and add the shortening. Pulse just until combined and the mixture still has a few pea-sized pieces of butter. Sprinkle 3 Tbsp of the ice water over the mixture and pulse until the dough just comes together. If the dough is still dry, add a bit more water as needed. Turn the dough out onto a large sheet of plastic wrap and press into a disk. Cover with another sheet of plastic wrap and, using a rolling pin, roll into a rough circle. Refrigerate until firm, 15–20 minutes.

Position a rack in the bottom third of the oven and preheat to 400°F (200°C). Line a baking sheet with parchment paper.

Remove the dough from the refrigerator and peel off the top sheet of plastic wrap. Dust the dough with flour and roll into a round about 13 inches (33 cm) in diameter. Transfer the dough round to the prepared baking sheet, cover, and refrigerate.

Place the squash on another baking sheet, drizzle with 1 Tbsp of the oil, and toss to coat. Spread in an even layer, season with salt, and roast until almost tender, about 10 minutes. Let cool.

In a frying pan, heat the remaining 1 Tbsp oil over medium-high heat. Add the chorizo and sauté until lightly browned, about 2 minutes. Transfer to paper towels to drain. Pour off all but 1½ Tbsp of the fat and return the pan to medium-high heat. Add the onion and sauté until tender, about 5 minutes. Season with salt, add the garlic, and cook for 1 minute. Let cool.

Remove the dough from the refrigerator. Spread evenly with the onion mixture, leaving a 1½-inch (4-cm) border. Evenly distribute the squash and chorizo over the onion mixture and sprinkle with the cheese. Fold the dough border up and over the filling, forming loose pleats. In a small bowl, lightly beat the egg yolk with 1 tsp water. Brush the dough border.

Bake until the crust is browned, about 30 minutes. Cut into wedges and serve.

serve with

Present a platter of Maple-Glazed Bacon (page 146) along with eggs, such as Baked Eggs with Spinach and Cream (page 79), and/or something sweet like steel-cut oats topped with fruit (page 40). At holiday time, serve mulled wine with cinnamon sticks.

Salads

dressings

Easy to make, vinaigrettes are a great way to add flair and flavor to your brunch salads. Choose ingredients that complement the season and occasion, mixing and matching the different components to create a memorable taste.

lemon and thyme vinaigrette

Grated lemon zest and juice of ½ lemon

½ cup (4 fl oz/125 ml) extra-virgin olive oil

¼ cup (2 fl oz/60 ml) white wine vinegar

1½ tsp fresh thyme leaves

Sea salt and freshly ground pepper

In a small bowl, whisk together the lemon zest and juice, oil, vinegar, and thyme, then whisk in salt and pepper to taste.

makes about 1 cup (8 fl oz/250 ml)

champagne and shallot vinaigrette

1 shallot, minced

½ cup (4 fl oz/125 ml) extra-virgin olive oil

¼ cup (2 fl oz/60 ml) Champagne or Prosecco

¼ cup (2 fl oz/60 ml) champagne vinegar

Sea salt and freshly ground pepper

In a small bowl, whisk together the shallot, oil, champagne, and vinegar, then whisk in salt and pepper to taste.

makes about 1 cup (8 fl oz/250 ml)

sesame-orange vinaigrette

3 Tbsp Asian sesame oil

2 Tbsp fresh orange juice

1 tsp finely chopped fresh chives

Sea salt and freshly ground pepper

In a small bowl, whisk together the oil, orange juice, and chives, then whisk in salt and pepper to taste.

makes about ⅓ cup (3 fl oz/80 ml)

olive-anchovy vinaigrette

2 Tbsp chopped pitted Niçoise olives

2 or 3 olive oil–packed anchovy fillets

5 Tbsp (2½ fl oz/75 ml) extra-virgin olive oil

3 Tbsp white wine vinegar

2 Tbsp finely chopped fresh chives

¾ tsp sugar

¼ tsp Dijon mustard

In a food processor, combine the olives and anchovies and process until smooth, about 10 seconds. Add the oil, vinegar, chives, sugar, and mustard and process until well blended and smooth, about 10 seconds.

makes about ¾ cup (6 fl oz/180 ml)

bacon vinaigrette

4 slices bacon

2 Tbsp red wine vinegar

1 shallot, finely minced

1 Tbsp Dijon mustard

1 tsp chopped fresh thyme

2 Tbsp extra-virgin olive oil, plus more if needed

In a large frying pan, cook the bacon over medium heat until crisp, 7–10 minutes. Transfer to paper towels to drain, then reserve for another use. Reserve the rendered fat in the pan.

In a small bowl, whisk together the vinegar, shallot, mustard, and thyme. Carefully pour the bacon fat through a fine-mesh sieve into a spouted measuring cup. Slowly whisk the bacon fat into the vinegar mixture until smooth and emulsified. Taste the dressing. If it is too strong, adjust with oil, ½ tsp at a time.

makes about ½ cup (4 fl oz/120 ml)

roasted tomato and basil vinaigrette

8 red or yellow ripe cherry tomatoes

Sea salt and freshly ground pepper

¼ cup (2 fl oz/60 ml) red wine vinegar

4 fresh basil leaves

½ cup (4 fl oz/125 ml) extra-virgin olive oil

Preheat the oven to 400°F (200°C). Place the tomatoes on a small rimmed baking sheet and season well with salt and pepper. Roast until the skins are well blistered and burst, about 25 minutes. Pour the vinegar over the tomatoes and roast for 5 minutes more. Remove from the oven and let cool completely.

Transfer the roasted tomatoes and vinegar to a food processor and add the basil and oil. Process until smooth, about 1 minute. Season to taste with salt and pepper.

makes about 1 cup (8 fl oz/250 ml)

When summer offers perfectly ripened stone fruits, burnished with a delectable rosy blush, I rush to grasp them while I can.

stone fruit salad with lime-mint sugar

¼ cup (2 oz/60 g) sugar

2 Tbsp minced fresh mint

2 tsp grated lime zest

2 peaches, pitted and cut into slices ½ inch (12 mm) thick

2 nectarines, pitted and cut into slices ½ inch (12 mm) thick

½ cantaloupe or other melon, seeded, peeled, and cut into ½-inch (12-mm) cubes or into long paper-thin slices

1 cup (6 oz/185 g) seedless grapes, halved

Juice of 1 lime

serves 4–6

In a small bowl, stir together the sugar, mint, and lime zest.

In a bowl, combine the peaches, nectarines, melon, and grapes. Drizzle the fruit with the lime juice and stir gently to coat. Sprinkle with the sugar mixture and turn the fruit once or twice to coat evenly.

Transfer to a serving bowl and serve.

serve with

Balance this simple salad with some cheese and a small helping of carbohydrates and protein for energy: the Cheesy Egg Sandwiches (page 82) are perfect. For a sweet option, add Walnut–Chocolate Chip Banana Bread (page 51).

The bright and pleasing combination of lemon, mint, and feta always makes me think of Greece: sun sparkling on crystal-clear water and a rustic table in the shade of a tree—the perfect setting for brunch.

shaved zucchini with lemon, mint, and feta

4 green or yellow zucchini, about 2 lb (1 kg)

4 Tbsp (2 fl oz/ 60 ml) extra-virgin olive oil

1 tsp grated lemon zest

¼ cup (⅛ oz/10 g) torn fresh mint leaves

5 oz (155 g) feta cheese, coarsely chopped

¼ tsp coarse sea salt

¼ tsp freshly ground pepper

serves 4–6

Trim the zucchini but do not peel; the skin will add color and texture. Using a sharp vegetable peeler, shave the zucchini lengthwise into long, thin strips, letting the strips fall into a bowl. (Don't worry if you are unable to shave the seedy cores; discard them or reserve for another use.)

In a small bowl, whisk together the oil and lemon zest. Drizzle over the zucchini. Add the mint, cheese, salt, and pepper to the bowl and toss gently. Adjust the seasonings. Transfer the salad to a serving bowl or platter and serve.

serve with

Continue the Mediterranean theme established with this zucchini salad with the Cured Fish Platter with Accompaniments (page 101) and decadent Orange Marmalade Bread and Butter Pudding (page 48).

Spinach is a wonderfully clean-tasting green with the ability to stand up to sweet, savory, and tart flavors. Here it is combined with bright red strawberries to add color and sweetness to your brunch table.

baby spinach salad with roasted strawberries

2 pt (1 lb/500 g) large strawberries, halved lengthwise

5 Tbsp (2½ fl oz/ 75 ml) extra-virgin olive oil

3½ tsp sugar

Salt and freshly ground pepper

3 Tbsp red wine vinegar

2 Tbsp fresh orange juice

2 tsp chopped fresh tarragon

1 cup (5½ oz/170 g) blanched almonds, toasted

9 cups (14 oz/440 g) baby spinach

5 oz (155 g) pecorino romano cheese, shredded

serves 6

Preheat the oven to 400°F (200°C).

Place the strawberries on a rimmed baking sheet. Drizzle with 2 Tbsp of the oil and sprinkle with 2 tsp of the sugar, ¼ tsp salt, and several grinds of pepper. Toss to coat the berries evenly, then spread in an even layer. Roast until softened, about 10 minutes. Let cool to room temperature.

In a small bowl, combine the vinegar, orange juice, tarragon, and the remaining 1½ tsp sugar. Add a generous ¼ tsp salt and a few grinds of pepper and whisk until the sugar dissolves. Slowly whisk in the remaining 3 Tbsp oil until well blended. Adjust the seasonings.

In a small bowl, stir together the almonds and ¼ tsp salt. In a large bowl, combine the spinach, ¼ tsp salt, and several grinds of pepper. Whisk the vinaigrette, drizzle about three-fourths of it over the spinach, and toss well (reserve the remaining vinaigrette for another use). Taste and add more vinaigrette if necessary, then adjust the seasonings.

Arrange the spinach on plates. Top with the roasted strawberries, sprinkle with the almonds and cheese, and serve.

serve with

Pair this healthful salad with a rich partner: a platter of crisp thick-cut applewood-smoked bacon is always a good choice when spinach is on the menu. Whip up some Buttermilk Blueberry Pancakes (page 23), or if time is short, choose a simple egg scramble (with plenty of cheese) and some buttered toast.

watercress and grapefruit salad

1 large Ruby Red grapefruit

1½ Tbsp fresh orange juice

1 Tbsp extra-virgin olive oil

2 tsp red wine vinegar

1 tsp grated orange zest

Salt and freshly ground pepper

2 cups (2 oz/60 g) watercress leaves

2 oz (60 g) fresh goat cheese, crumbled

3 Tbsp hazelnuts, toasted and chopped

serves 4

Cut a thin slice off the top and bottom of the grapefruit, and stand the fruit on a cut end. Working from top to bottom, cut away the peel and white pith in wide strips, following the contour of the fruit. Working over a bowl, cut along both sides of each segment to free it from the membrane, capturing the segments in the bowl.

In a small bowl, whisk together the orange juice, oil, vinegar, and orange zest. Season with salt and pepper. Add the grapefruit segments and juice to the dressing, turning the segments gently to coat.

Place the watercress in a bowl and add enough of the vinaigrette to coat the leaves. Lift the grapefruit segments from the vinaigrette and add to the salad. Sprinkle with the goat cheese and hazelnuts and toss gently, adding more vinaigrette if necessary.

Arrange the salad on plates and serve.

serve with

For a California-inspired menu, serve Avocado, Bacon, and Tomato Tartines (page 92) with this pure and simple salad, then add sweetness with Ginger-Apricot Muffins (page 43).

easy drinking

The ruby red Italian aperitif Campari is a classic partner for grapefruit. Make a crisp, light, low-alcohol cocktail by combining one-third Campari and two-thirds sparkling water in a tall glass of ice. Top it off with a sprig of mint.

I sometimes ask myself if burrata—a thin sheet of fresh mozzarella wrapped around bits of mozzarella and cream—is simply too decadent, even for me. The answer is always the same: no.

nectarines with arugula and burrata

2 cups (2 oz/60 g) baby arugula

3 nectarines, pitted and cut into slices ½ inch (12 mm) thick

½ lb (250 g) *burrata* cheese

Extra-virgin olive oil for drizzling

Coarse salt and freshly ground pepper

Crusty bread, sliced, for serving

serves 6

Arrange the arugula on a large board or a serving platter. Scatter the nectarine slices evenly over the top. Place the cheese in a small bowl or directly on the platter. Drizzle with oil and sprinkle with salt and pepper.

Serve with slices of bread, letting diners layer the arugula, nectarines, and cheese on the bread.

serve with

When menu building, think color and texture along with sweet, savory, and tart. Here, for example, you might serve Raspberry-Lemon Muffins (page 36) for the sweet element and Easy Eggs Benedict (page 89) for a savory option.

I first encountered the inspired pairing of cool watermelon and feta cheese while working on a book with a talented Greek chef. Ever since, this dish has been a favorite addition to my table.

watermelon and shaved celery with feta

6 celery stalks

1 small seedless watermelon, about 3¾ lb (1.7 kg)

5–6 oz (155–185 g) feta cheese, coarsely crumbled

1 cup (1 oz/30 g) torn fresh mint leaves

¼ cup (2 fl oz/60 ml) extra-virgin olive oil

1 Tbsp fresh lemon juice

1 tsp salt

¼ tsp freshly ground pepper

serves 4–6

If the celery stalks are fibrous, use a vegetable peeler to remove the stringy outer layer. Using the peeler, shave the stalks into long, thin strips. If the stalks become too thin to shave, slice them as thinly as possible with a chef's knife.

Cut the watermelon in half through the stem end. Cut each half in half again to make quarters. Cut the flesh from the rind of each quarter, carefully following the curve of the rind. Cut the flesh into ¾-inch (2-cm) cubes. Alternatively, cut off a thin slice from the top and bottom of the watermelon to reveal the flesh, then cut the watermelon crosswise into thin slices. Trim away the rind from each slice. Using round cookie or biscuit cutters in various sizes, cut the melon flesh into rounds.

In a large bowl, combine the celery, watermelon, feta, and mint. Drizzle with the oil and lemon juice, sprinkle with the salt and pepper, and toss to mix well. Adjust the seasonings. Using a slotted spoon, arrange the salad on plates and serve.

serve with

Spring Vegetable Frittata (page 72) would make the ideal partner for this fresh and bright salad with its crunch and slight tanginess. To add a sweet note, make a batch of cinnamon toast with plenty of good butter and brown sugar, or bake Cinnamon Rolls with Cream Cheese Icing (page 56).

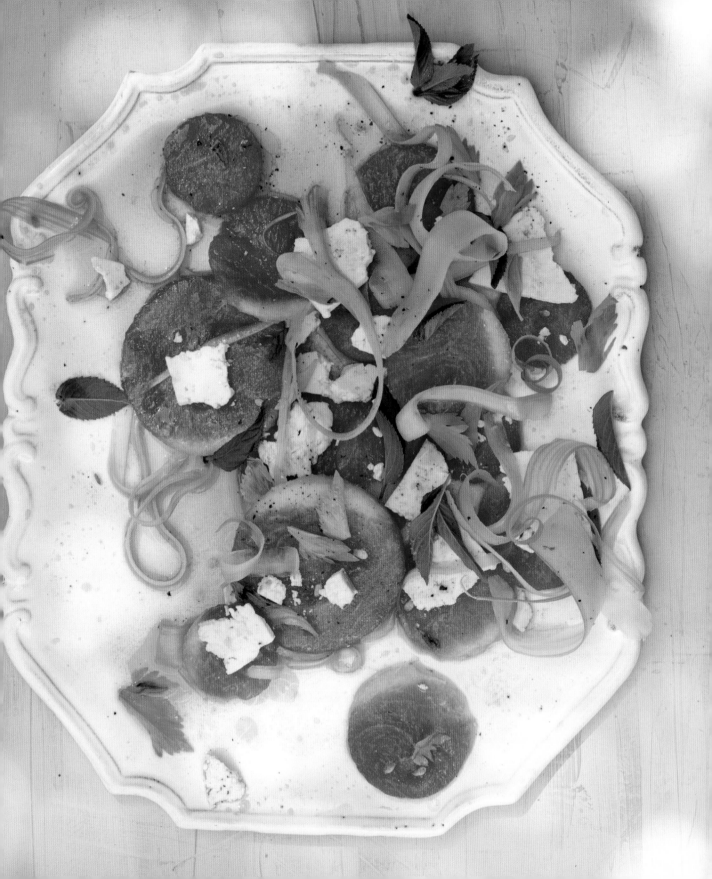

salade niçoise with seared salmon

for the vinaigrette

2 Tbsp chopped pitted Niçoise olives

3 olive oil–packed anchovy fillets

5 Tbsp (2½ oz/75 g) extra-virgin olive oil

3 Tbsp white wine vinegar

2 Tbsp finely chopped fresh chives

¾ tsp sugar

¼ tsp Dijon mustard

2 lb (1 kg) small red potatoes, quartered

Salt and freshly ground pepper

Ice water

¾ lb (375 g) haricots verts

6 skinless wild salmon fillets, 5–6 oz (155–185 g) each, pin bones removed

1 Tbsp canola oil

1 head romaine lettuce

3½ cups (21 oz/655 g) grape tomatoes, halved lengthwise

6 large eggs, hardboiled, peeled, and quartered

2 Tbsp finely chopped fresh chives

Niçoise olives for serving

serves 6

To make the vinaigrette, in a food processor, combine the olives and anchovies and process until smooth, about 10 seconds. Add the oil, vinegar, chives, sugar, and mustard and process until a smooth dressing forms, about 10 seconds.

In a large saucepan, combine the potatoes, 1 Tbsp salt, and water to cover, and bring to a boil over high heat. Reduce the heat to medium, cover partially, and simmer until the potatoes are just tender, 5–7 minutes. Drain the potatoes, transfer to a large bowl of ice water, and let cool. Using a slotted spoon, transfer the potatoes to a large bowl. Reserve the ice water, adding more ice if needed to cool it down.

Fill the same saucepan with water and bring to a boil. Add 1 Tbsp salt and the haricots verts and cook until tender-crisp, about 2 minutes. Drain the haricots verts, transfer to the ice water, and let cool. Drain well and transfer to a second bowl.

Season the salmon fillets on both sides with salt and pepper. In a large frying pan, warm the oil over medium-high heat until very hot but not smoking. Working in batches, add the fillets, skinned side up, and cook until golden brown, about 2 minutes. Turn and cook until just opaque at the center, 2–3 minutes. Transfer to a large plate and tent with aluminum foil.

Seperate the romaine leaves from the head and reserve the large leaves for another use. Put the lettuce leaves in a bowl. Lightly dress the lettuce, potatoes, and green beans with the vinaigrette, using only about half of the total vinaigrette. In a bowl, toss the tomatoes with about ¼ tsp salt.

Divide the lettuce leaves among plates, placing them to one side. Using a slotted spoon, place the tomatoes on the lettuce, dividing them evenly. Divide the salmon, beans, potatoes, and egg quarters evenly among the plates, and sprinkle the eggs lightly with salt. Add several olives to each plate, garnish the fish and vegetables with the chives, and serve. Pass the remaining vinaigrette at the table.

serve with

This classic salad has it all—protein, carbohydrates, and vegetables. For a simple brunch, it can stand alone. For a more extensive menu, accompany it with Corn Fritters (page 148) or Ginger-Apricot Muffins (page 79) and a big pitcher of Summer Fruit Rosé Sangria (page 165).

Here is a rustic, elemental salad that will ready anyone for the rigors of a lazy Sunday afternoon. When the soft yellow yolk breaks and runs into the pleasingly tart vinaigrette, lightly coating the greens and bacon, all the flavors come together.

warm escarole, egg, and bacon salad

2 heads escarole

3 Tbsp extra-virgin olive oil

2 Tbsp red wine vinegar

½ tsp salt

⅛ tsp freshly ground pepper

6 slices bacon, cut into ½-inch (12-mm) pieces

1 tsp fresh lemon juice

4 large eggs

serves 4

Remove the outer dark green leaves from each head of escarole and reserve for another use. Separate the inner pale yellow leaves. You should have 5 cups (15 oz/470 g). Tear the leaves into bite-sized pieces.

In a large bowl, whisk together the oil, vinegar, salt, and pepper. Add the escarole, but do not toss.

In a frying pan, sauté the bacon over medium heat until crisp, 4–5 minutes. Using a slotted spoon, transfer to paper towels to drain briefly. Add the bacon to the bowl, toss the salad, and arrange on plates or in shallow bowls.

Pour water to a depth of 2 inches (5 cm) into a large, deep sauté pan and add the lemon juice. Bring to a gentle simmer over medium-low heat. One at a time, crack the eggs into a ramekin or small cup and gently slide into the simmering water. Cook until the whites are set and the yolks are glazed over but still soft, 4–5 minutes. Using a slotted spoon, lift each egg from the simmering water, draining well and blotting the bottom of each egg briefly on paper towels. Trim any ragged edges of egg white with kitchen scissors.

Top each salad with a poached egg and serve.

serve with

The only real accompaniments this immensely appealing dish needs are a batch of Balsamic Bloody Marys (page 160) and a stack of buttered brioche toast. Or, if you want to skip the alcoholic beverage, serve Spiced Iced Coffee (page 167).

roasted beet salad with blue cheese, grapefruit, and tarragon

3 large beets in assorted colors

3 large ruby red grapefruits

1 Tbsp raspberry or red wine vinegar

1 tsp honey

Salt and freshly ground pepper

¼ cup (2 fl oz/ 60 ml) extra-virgin olive oil

2 heads frisée, leaves torn into bite-sized pieces

6 oz (185 g) blue cheese, such as Maytag, crumbled

2½ Tbsp chopped fresh tarragon

serves 6

Preheat the oven to 400°F (200°C).

Wrap the beets in aluminum foil and place on a baking sheet. Roast until tender when pierced with a knife, about 1 hour and 10 minutes. Remove from the oven, unwrap, and let cool. Slip off the skins and discard. Cut the beets crosswise into slices about ¼ inch (6 mm) thick and then cut each slice into quarters.

Cut a thin slice off the top and bottom of each grapefruit and stand the fruit on a cut end. Working from top to bottom, cut away the peel and white pith in wide strips, following the contour of the fruit. Working over a bowl, cut along both sides of each segment to free it from the membrane, capturing the fragments in the bowl. Squeeze the membranes to extract any additional juice.

Place ⅓ cup (3 fl oz/80 ml) of the grapefruit juice in a small bowl (reserve the remainder for another use). Whisk in the vinegar, honey, ¼ tsp salt, and several grinds of pepper. Slowly whisk in the oil until well blended. Adjust the seasonings.

In a large bowl, toss the frisée with ¼ tsp salt and several grinds of pepper. Whisk the dressing and then drizzle about one-fourth of it over the frisée and toss well. Adjust the seasonings.

Mound the frisée on plates. Top with the grapefruit segments and beets. Drizzle each serving with 1 tsp of the remaining dressing (reserve the remainder for another use). Sprinkle with the blue cheese and tarragon, and serve.

serve with

Gingerbread-Spiced Apple Pancakes (page 31) will make a fantastic complement to this dish. For a more bountiful table, offer a big platter of crisp, sweet Maple-Glazed Bacon (page 146).

bread salad with charred tomatoes, cucumber, and olives

½ loaf country-style Italian bread, such as Pugliese, cut into ½-inch (12-mm) cubes

4 large ripe tomatoes, preferably in a mix of colors, about 2½ lb (1.25 kg)

1 small English cucumber, halved lengthwise and seeds removed

½ red onion, diced

¾ cup (3 oz/90 g) Kalamata olives, pitted and coarsely chopped

⅓ cup (3 fl oz/80 ml) extra-virgin olive oil

2 Tbsp red wine vinegar

Salt and freshly ground pepper

Leaves from ½ bunch fresh basil, torn into small pieces

serves 4

Preheat the oven to 375°F (190°C).

Place the bread cubes in a single layer on a baking sheet. Lightly toast in the oven until the cubes are just dry and very light brown, 8–10 minutes. Remove the cubes from the sheet.

Preheat the broiler. Line the baking sheet with aluminum foil and place the tomatoes on the prepared sheet. Broil 6 inches (15 cm) from the heat source until the skins begin to char and blacken, 2–3 minutes. Turn the tomatoes and broil for 2–3 minutes more. Remove from the oven and let cool. Remove and discard any loose skin. Coarsely chop the tomatoes and transfer to a large bowl.

Cut the cucumber halves crosswise into slices about ½ inch (12 mm) thick and add to the bowl. Add the onion, olives, oil, and vinegar. Season with salt and pepper and stir well. Cover and let stand at room temperature for up to 1 hour to blend the flavors.

Add the toasted bread cubes and toss gently. Add the basil leaves and toss gently. Adjust the seasonings and serve.

serve with

Round out this hearty dish with Polenta with Poached Eggs, Prosciutto, and Pecorino (page 87). If your guests are likely to crave a sweet note, keep it light by adding a generous bowl of fresh strawberries tossed with Demerara sugar. For drinks, serve up Micheladas (page 160) or Virgin Marys.

meyer lemon–crab salad with mango

2 Meyer lemons

1½ lb (750 g) lump
crabmeat, picked
over for shells

¾ cup (6 fl oz/180 ml)
mayonnaise

Salt and freshly
ground pepper

½ tsp sugar

2 Tbsp extra-virgin
olive oil

2 mangoes

1 large head red leaf
lettuce, leaves torn
into bite-sized pieces

4 green onions, white
and light green parts,
thinly sliced

serves 6

Finely grate the zest of 1 of the lemons. Halve both lemons and extract enough juice to measure 5 Tbsp (3 fl oz/80 ml).

In a bowl, combine the crabmeat, mayonnaise, lemon zest, 4 Tbsp (2 fl oz/60 ml) of the lemon juice, ¾ tsp salt, and ½ tsp pepper. Stir gently to mix. Adjust the seasonings.

In a small bowl, whisk together the remaining 1 Tbsp lemon juice, the sugar, ⅛ tsp salt, and several grinds of pepper until the sugar dissolves. Slowly whisk in the oil until well blended. Adjust the seasonings.

Stand 1 mango on one of its narrow sides, with the stem end facing you. Using a sharp knife, and positioning it about 1 inch (2.5 cm) from the stem, cut down the length of the fruit, just brushing the pit. Repeat on the other side of the pit. Hold each half cut side up and score the flesh to make pieces about 1½ inches (4 cm) long and ¼ inch (6 mm) thick and stopping just short of the skin. Push against the skin side of the half to force the pieces outward, then cut across the base of the pieces to free them. Repeat with the second mango.

In a large bowl, toss the lettuce with a pinch of salt and a few grinds of pepper. Whisk the dressing, drizzle it over the lettuce, and toss well. Arrange the lettuce on plates. Top each serving with a spoonful of the crab mixture. Scatter the mango pieces around the crab. Sprinkle with the green onions and serve.

serve with
Keep the momentum of the menu rolling with sophisticated Brioche French Toast with Figs (page 24). If the morning feast is likely to stretch into the afternoon, open up a classic buttery-oaky Chardonnay from California or a crisp Sauvignon Blanc to pair with the crab.

fattoush with shredded roast chicken

Olive oil for frying

1 large pita bread, torn into bite-sized pieces

1 heart romaine lettuce, cored and chopped

1 cup (2 oz/60 g) purslane, chopped

1 cup (6 oz/185 g) cherry tomatoes, halved lengthwise

1 cucumber, peeled, seeded, and diced

⅛ cup (1 oz/30 g) very thinly sliced red onion

3 Tbsp chopped fresh mint

2 Tbsp chopped fresh flat-leaf parsley

2 oz (60 g) *ricotta salata* cheese, coarsely grated

½ tsp ground sumac, plus more for garnish

2 cups (10 oz/315 g) shredded roast chicken

for the dressing

3 Tbsp fresh lemon juice

¼ tsp ground sumac

Salt and freshly ground pepper

¼ cup (2 fl oz/60 ml) extra-virgin olive oil

serves 6

Pour oil to a depth of 1 inch (2.5 cm) into a large frying pan and heat over medium-high heat. Add some of the pita pieces; be sure not to crowd the pan. Fry, turning once, until golden brown, about 1 minute. Transfer to paper towels to drain. Repeat with the remaining pita pieces. Let cool completely.

In a large bowl, combine the lettuce, purslane, tomatoes, cucumber, onion, mint, parsley, *ricotta salata*, and ½ tsp sumac.

To make the dressing, in a small bowl, whisk together the lemon juice, sumac, and salt and pepper to taste. Add the oil in a slow, steady stream, whisking constantly.

Add the pita pieces to the salad and drizzle half of the dressing over the top. Toss to mix well.

Add more dressing if needed (refrigerate the remaining dressing for another use). Transfer the salad to a platter and top with the shredded chicken. Lightly sprinkle with sumac and serve.

serve with

The addition of chicken makes this a filling dish on its own. For a more festive table, add a pomegranate juice "cocktail" (combine equal parts bottled pomegranate juice and sparkling water or grapefruit soda over lots of ice) and Sweet Almond Buns with Cardamom (page 58).

grilled shrimp salad with avocado and chipotle dressing

⅓ cup (3 fl oz/ 80 ml) plus 1 Tbsp mayonnaise

¾ cup (¾ oz/20 g) coarsely chopped fresh cilantro

2⅓ Tbsp fresh lime juice

1½ Tbsp fresh orange juice

1 small shallot, minced

1 Tbsp chipotle chiles in adobo sauce, seeded and minced, plus 1½ Tbsp adobo sauce

Salt and freshly ground pepper

1½ lb (750 g) large shrimp, peeled and deveined

1 can (15 oz/470 g) black beans, drained and rinsed

1 large head romaine lettuce, leaves torn into bite-sized pieces

2 avocados, halved, pitted, peeled, and cut lengthwise into slices about ⅜ inch (1 cm) thick

serves 6–8

In a food processor, combine the mayonnaise, half of the cilantro, 2 tsp of the lime juice, the orange juice, shallot, chiles, ¼ tsp salt, and several grinds of pepper. Process until a creamy, smooth dressing forms, about 10 seconds. Adjust the seasonings. Cover and refrigerate until needed.

Soak 12 bamboo skewers in water to cover for at least 30 minutes. Prepare a charcoal or gas grill for direct-heat grilling over high heat. Oil the grill rack.

In a bowl, combine the shrimp, 1 Tbsp of the lime juice, and 1 Tbsp of the adobo sauce and toss to coat evenly. Let stand at room temperature for 15 minutes to blend the flavors.

In a small bowl, combine the beans, the remaining 1½ tsp adobo sauce, ½ tsp of the lime juice, ¼ tsp salt, and a few grinds of pepper. Let stand at room temperature for 15 minutes to blend the flavors.

Drain the skewers and thread 3 or 4 shrimp onto each skewer. Sprinkle lightly with salt and pepper and grill, turning once, until the shrimp are pink and opaque throughout, 3–5 minutes. Transfer to a plate and sprinkle the shrimp with the remaining 2 tsp lime juice. Slide the shrimp off the skewers.

In a large bowl, toss the lettuce with ¼ tsp salt and several grinds of pepper. Arrange on plates and top with the black beans, shrimp, and avocado slices. Drizzle each salad with about 2 Tbsp of the dressing and sprinkle with 1 Tbsp of the remaining cilantro, then serve.

serve with

This south-of-the-border dish is a brightly colored, spicy collection of all the best things Mexico has to offer a hungry brunch guest. This seafood salad screams for a Michelada (page 160) or Cantaloupe Agua Fresca (page 163). Add a Blackberry Coffee Cake (page 35) and your menu is complete.

A perfect dish to serve at a garden brunch under dappled sunlight, this salad achieves perfection when made with sweet Vidalias and spicy wild arugula.

arugula and fennel salad with black pepper–crusted tuna

¼ cup (2 fl oz/60 ml) balsamic vinegar

1 large shallot, minced

2 tsp Dijon mustard

½ tsp sugar

Salt

10 Tbsp (6 fl oz/ 180 ml) extra-virgin olive oil

2 small Vidalia onions, thinly sliced

2 Tbsp peppercorns

6 tuna steaks, 2 lb (1 kg) total, each about 1 inch (2.5 cm) thick

8 cups (½ lb/250 g) arugula leaves

1 large fennel bulb, cored and thinly sliced

2 green onions, green tops only, thinly sliced

serves 6

In a small bowl, combine the vinegar, shallot, mustard, and sugar. Add ¼ tsp salt and whisk until the sugar dissolves. Slowly whisk in 7 Tbsp (3½ oz/105 ml) of the oil until well blended. Adjust the seasonings.

In a large frying pan, heat 2 Tbsp of the oil over medium heat. Add the sliced onions and 1 tsp salt and sauté until softened and browned, 10–12 minutes. Transfer to a plate. Wipe the pan clean and set aside.

Place the peppercorns in a resealable plastic bag and seal closed. Using a mallet or the bottom of a small, heavy pan, coarsely crack the peppercorns. Season the tuna steaks on both sides with a little salt. Press the cracked peppercorns into one side of each steak.

Heat the remaining 1 Tbsp oil in the frying pan over medium-high heat. When the oil is hot but not smoking, add the tuna, peppered side down. Sear, turning once, until lightly golden on the outside and still dark pink in the center, or rare, about 2 minutes on each side, or until cooked to your liking. Transfer to a platter, tent with aluminum foil, and let rest for 5 minutes.

In a large bowl, toss together the arugula, fennel, and ¼ tsp salt. Whisk the vinaigrette, drizzle about half of it over the arugula mixture, and toss well. Adjust the seasonings. Arrange the arugula mixture on plates and top with the sautéed onions. Thinly slice each tuna steak and arrange on the onions. Drizzle each salad with some of the remaining vinaigrette. Sprinkle with the green onion tops and serve.

serve with

Since this dish features tuna and green vegetables, all you need to round out the menu is a starchy side and/or a sweet treat. To play up the garden theme, serve Roasted Red Pepper and Potato Frittata (page 73) and Lemon-Ricotta Pancakes with Compote (page 25).

quinoa with tomatoes, cucumber, and fresh herbs

1½ cups (5½ oz/ 170 g) quinoa, rinsed and drained

3 cups (24 fl oz/ 750 ml) chicken or vegetable broth

Salt and freshly ground pepper

2 large lemons

2 cloves garlic, minced

1 Tbsp pomegranate molasses

1 tsp sugar

½ cup (4 fl oz/ 125 ml) extra-virgin olive oil

2 large tomatoes, cored, seeded, and cut into ½-inch (12-mm) dice

½ large English cucumber, cut into ½-inch (12-mm) dice

4 green onions, white and light green parts, thinly sliced

¼ cup (⅛ oz/10 g) coarsely chopped fresh flat-leaf parsley

¼ cup (⅛ oz/10 g) coarsely chopped fresh mint

serves 4–6

In a saucepan, combine the quinoa, the broth, and ¼ tsp salt and bring to a boil over high heat. Cover, reduce the heat to medium-low, and simmer until all the liquid is absorbed and the quinoa is tender, about 12 minutes. Transfer the quinoa to a fine-mesh sieve and rinse with cold running water until cool, 1–2 minutes. Drain well and transfer to a bowl.

Finely grate the zest from 1 of the lemons. Halve both lemons and extract enough juice to measure 5 Tbsp (3 fl oz/80 ml). In a small bowl, whisk together the lemon juice and zest, garlic, pomegranate molasses, sugar, ½ tsp salt, and several grinds of pepper until the sugar dissolves. Slowly whisk in the oil until well blended. Adjust the seasonings. Add about three-fourths of the dressing to the quinoa and stir well.

In a small bowl, toss the tomatoes with ¼ tsp salt. Let stand until they release their juice, about 5 minutes. Pour into a sieve set over a bowl. Place the cucumber in the bowl used to season the tomatoes. Add the green onions and the remaining dressing, toss well, and pour over the tomatoes in the sieve to drain.

Add the drained tomato-cucumber mixture to the quinoa. Stir in the parsley and mint, adjust the seasonings, and serve.

serve with

To balance the menu, add protein with a Sausage and Cheddar Strata (page 81); for a simple sweet note, serve sliced plums and nectarines, or prepare a Nectarine-Almond Oven Pancake (page 26). Pour glasses of freshly squeezed tangerine juice to add the final piece to the nutritional puzzle.

Sides

Serving citrus at brunch sets the tone for a nutritious and light menu—and energizes your guests for the day. It's perfect before a long bike ride, hike, or sail.

broiled grapefruit with brown sugar

3 grapefruits, halved

6 Tbsp (2⅓ oz/75 g) firmly packed light brown sugar

serves 6

Preheat the broiler. Line a baking sheet with aluminum foil.

Arrange the grapefruit halves, cut sides up, on the prepared sheet. Sprinkle each half with 1 Tbsp of the sugar. Place in the broiler about 4 inches (10 cm) from the heat source. Broil until the sugar has melted and is bubbling, 2–3 minutes. Transfer to bowls or a platter and serve at once.

serve with

Balance the menu with protein, in the form of sizzled ham, sausage, or bacon. Add Maple-Coconut Granola with Yogurt and Mango (page 39) to create a filling yet not too heavy meal.

The sweet and creamy flavors in this lovely dish are the perfect vehicle for summer's bounty of fruit. Mix and match the stone fruits as desired.

oven-roasted fruit with ricotta cream

1 cup (8 oz/250 g) whole-milk ricotta cheese

¼ cup (2 oz/60 g) crème fraîche

½ tsp pure vanilla extract

6 Tbsp (3 oz/90 g) sugar

2 peaches

2 nectarines

3 plums

8 fresh figs

About ½ lb (250 g) cherries (optional)

1 Tbsp olive oil

Honey for serving

serves 6–8

Preheat the oven to 475°F (245°C). In a bowl, combine the ricotta, crème fraîche, vanilla, and 2 Tbsp of the sugar and mix well. Cover and refrigerate until ready to use.

Halve the peaches, nectarines, and plums and remove the pits. Cut the halves in half again, if desired. Trim off the hard tip of each fig stem and leave the figs whole. Leave the cherries whole, if using. Combine all the fruits in a roasting pan large enough to hold them in a single layer, drizzle with the oil, and turn to coat. Sprinkle with the remaining 4 Tbsp (2 oz/60 g) sugar and turn once or twice. Spread the fruit in an even layer.

Roast until the fruits are slightly collapsed and golden or lightly charred, 15–20 minutes.

Spoon the fruits and their cooking juices into bowls. Halve or quarter the figs lengthwise, if desired. If using the cherries, let diners know that the pits are intact. Swirl a little honey into the ricotta mixture and serve with the fruit.

serve with

Complement this sweet dish with savory eggs like Fried Eggs with Asparagus, Pancetta, and Bread Crumbs (page 67). Add a batch of Honey-Tangerine Fizzes (page 159) to round out this cozy menu.

turkey and yukon gold hash

1 lb (500 g) Yukon gold potatoes of uniform size

Salt and freshly ground pepper

About 3 Tbsp canola oil

1 lb (500 g) ground turkey

2 Tbsp chopped fresh sage

1 green bell pepper, seeded and finely chopped

⅔ cup (3 oz/90 g) chopped yellow onion

serves 4

Place the potatoes in a saucepan, add 2 tsp salt and water to cover by 2 inches (5 cm), and bring to a boil over high heat. Reduce the heat to medium, cover, and cook until the potatoes can be easily pierced with a fork, 35–40 minutes. Drain and let cool, then peel the potatoes and cut into ¼-inch (6-mm) cubes.

In a frying pan, warm 1 Tbsp of the oil over high heat. Add the ground turkey, sage, ½ tsp salt, and ¼ tsp pepper. Sauté until browned, 7–8 minutes. Using a slotted spoon, transfer the turkey to paper towels to drain. Leave the fat in the pan.

In a bowl, combine the turkey, potatoes, and bell pepper. Add enough oil to the pan to total 2 Tbsp fat and heat over medium-high heat. Add the onion and sauté until softened, 2–3 minutes. Layer the turkey mixture on top of the onion and press flat with a spatula. Season with salt and pepper. Cook, without turning, until a brown crust forms on the bottom, 15–20 minutes.

Remove from the heat and invert a large, flat platter on top of the pan. Using pot holders, hold both pan and platter firmly and invert them together. Lift off the pan, exposing the crusty bottom of the hash. Cut into wedges and serve.

serve with

Include other American favorites on the menu, like Easy Eggs Benedict (page 89). Add freshly squeezed juice and Walnut–Chocolate Chip Banana Bread (page 51).

Adding celery root to the classic potato pancake lightens the texture and adds a pleasing nutty flavor. Dress up this dish with a dollop of crème fraîche and caviar.

potato–celery root pancakes

2 small russet potatoes, about 1 lb (500 g), peeled

1 celery root, about ½ lb (250 g), peeled

2 shallots, minced

2 large eggs

2 Tbsp all-purpose flour

1½ tsp salt

1½ tsp freshly ground pepper

Canola oil for cooking

Coarse sea salt

serves 4–6

Using a food processor fitted with the shredding disk or the large holes of a box grater-shredder, shred the potatoes and celery root. Line a colander with cheesecloth. Transfer the potatoes and celery root to the colander, set over a bowl, and twist the cheesecloth tightly into a pouch, squeezing out the moisture. Let the vegetables drain for 15 minutes. Squeeze the cheesecloth again. Carefully pour the clear liquid from the bowl, leaving behind the white starchy substance that settles at the bottom.

Add the shallots, eggs, flour, salt, and pepper to the bowl and beat with a fork until well blended. Add the shredded potatoes and celery root and toss to combine.

Line a baking sheet with paper towels. Pour oil to a depth of ¼ inch (6 mm) into a large, deep frying pan and heat over medium-high heat. When the oil begins to shimmer, carefully drop heaping tablespoonfuls of the potato mixture into the pan, spacing them about 1 inch (2.5 cm) apart. Using a spatula, gently press on the pancakes to flatten them and cook until they are golden and crisp on the first sides, 3–4 minutes. Turn and cook until golden and crisp on the second sides, 3–4 minutes. Transfer the pancakes to the towel–lined sheet to drain. Repeat to cook the remaining potato mixture. Sprinkle the pancakes with coarse sea salt and serve.

serve with

Pair with a salty protein—perhaps spiral-sliced ham or sausages—then round out the menu with Cajun Scramble (page 86) and orange slices or grapefruit halves.

sautéed tomatoes with arugula pesto and feta

3 Tbsp walnuts

Grated zest
of 1 lemon

1 clove garlic,
coarsely chopped

Leaves from ¼ bunch
fresh basil

1 cup (1 oz/30 g)
packed baby arugula
leaves, plus more for
serving (optional)

5 Tbsp (3 fl oz/80 ml)
extra-virgin olive oil

Salt and freshly
ground pepper

1½ lb (750 g)
pear tomatoes

2 oz (60 g)
feta cheese

serves 4

Preheat the oven to 375°F (190°C). Spread the walnuts in a baking pan. Toast until they turn a shade or two darker and are fragrant, 6–8 minutes. Pour the nuts onto a plate to cool.

In a food processor, combine the toasted walnuts, lemon zest, and garlic and pulse just to combine. Add the basil and arugula and process until coarsely chopped. With the motor running, slowly pour in 4 Tbsp (2 fl oz/60 ml) of the oil. Continue to process until the mixture is moist and well blended but still slightly chunky. Transfer the pesto to a small bowl and adjust the seasonings with salt and pepper.

In a frying pan, warm the remaining 1 Tbsp oil over medium-high heat. Add the tomatoes and a pinch of salt and sauté until the tomatoes are warmed through and their skins are just beginning to split, 3–4 minutes. Remove from the heat and stir in the pesto. Transfer the tomatoes to a serving dish and crumble the cheese over the top. Serve hot or at room temperature. If desired, top the tomatoes and cheese with a scattering of arugula leaves.

serve with

This colorful and flavorful side pairs well with a sophisticated main dish such as crab cakes (page 102), or even Steak and Eggs (page 96). Add Grapefruit-Prosecco Sparklers (page 162), for a festive touch.

Simple side dishes can transform your brunch menu and are an opportunity to make the most of fresh seasonal ingredients. Here, small, sweet tomatoes and tangy feta dressed with an arugula pesto show off summer's crops.

hash browns

1 Tbsp unsalted butter

1 yellow onion, chopped

1 green or red bell pepper, seeded and chopped

Salt and freshly ground pepper

3 large russet potatoes, about 1½ lb (750 g), peeled

4 Tbsp (2 fl oz/60 ml) canola oil

serves 4

In a heavy frying pan, preferably cast iron, melt the butter over medium heat. Add the onion and bell pepper and cook, stirring occasionally, until tender, about 10 minutes. Season with salt and pepper. Transfer to a bowl.

Using a food processor fitted with the shredding disk or the large holes of a box grater-shredder, shred the potatoes. Line a colander with cheesecloth and set the colander in the sink or over a bowl. Transfer the potatoes to the colander and twist the cheesecloth tightly into a pouch, squeezing out the moisture. Let the potatoes drain for 15 minutes. Squeeze the cheesecloth again, then transfer the potatoes back to a large bowl. Add 1½ tsp salt and ¼ tsp pepper and mix well.

In the same frying pan, heat 2 Tbsp of the oil over medium-high heat. Add the potato mixture and spread into a thick cake. Reduce the heat to medium, cover, and cook until golden brown and crisp, about 6 minutes. Using a wide metal spatula, slide the potato cake onto a plate. Heat the remaining 2 Tbsp oil in the pan. Carefully flip the potato cake, browned side up, into the pan. Cook until golden brown and crisp on the second side, about 6 minutes.

Slide the potatoes onto a platter. Return the onion mixture to the pan and cook, stirring often, until reheated, about 1 minute. Heap the onion mixture onto the potatoes and serve.

serve with

Hash browns are such a classic component of the morning table that they can be paired with almost any balanced combo of protein, fruit, and sweet. Remember that potatoes will discolor over time, so choose simple or make-ahead dishes that will allow you to concentrate on shredding and cooking the potatoes not too long before serving time.

Your guests will be impressed that you've made your own sausage (little do they know how easy it is!). Season the patties with a combination of herbs to suit the season.

sausage patties

2 Tbsp dried bread crumbs

2 tsp minced fresh sage or 1 tsp dried sage

1 tsp minced fresh rosemary or ½ tsp dried rosemary

1 tsp minced fresh thyme or ½ tsp dried thyme

¼ tsp red pepper flakes

Pinch of ground cloves

Pinch of freshly grated nutmeg

1¾ tsp salt

½ tsp freshly ground pepper

1½ lb (750 g) ground pork

1 Tbsp pure maple syrup

serves 6

In a large bowl, stir together the bread crumbs, sage, rosemary, thyme, red pepper flakes, cloves, nutmeg, salt, and pepper. Add the ground pork and maple syrup. Mix gently with your hands until just combined. Cover and refrigerate for 30–45 minutes.

Shape the pork mixture into 6 patties, each about 3 inches (7.5 cm) in diameter. Heat a large frying pan, preferably nonstick, over medium heat. Add the patties and reduce the heat to medium-low. Cook until browned, about 5 minutes. Turn and cook until browned on the second sides and the centers feel firm when pressed with a finger, about 5 minutes. Serve hot.

serve with

Offer a surprisingly easy (but very impressive) dish like Nectarine-Almond Oven Pancake (page 26). Add a bright and crisp vegetable-centric element, such as Shaved Zucchini with Lemon, Mint, and Feta (page 112).

variation

Try substituting half of the ground pork with ground beef round. Add a small clove of garlic, minced, if you'd like.

I like making sausage from scratch because I can adjust the flavorings to taste. Make notes so you can keep improving on the recipe, and freeze your experiments for an easy addition to an impromptu brunch.

chicken-apple sausages

1½ lb (750 g) boneless, skinless chicken breasts, frozen for 1 hour

¼ lb (125 g) sliced bacon, frozen for 1 hour

1 Tbsp unsalted butter

2 Granny Smith apples, peeled, cored, grated, and squeezed dry

2 tsp coriander seeds

1 tsp fennel seeds

2 tsp white or black peppercorns

½ tsp salt

½ tsp freshly grated nutmeg

¼ tsp cayenne pepper

2 Tbsp olive oil

serves 6–8

Working in batches, place the chicken in a food processor and pulse until coarsely ground, 6 to 8 times. Transfer to a large bowl. Pulse the bacon until coarsely ground, 3 or 4 times. Add the bacon and the butter to the chicken and mix until well blended. Add the apples.

In a spice mill or in a mortar with a pestle, grind the coriander seeds, fennel seeds, and peppercorns to a medium-fine grind. Add the spices to the chicken mixture along with the salt, nutmeg, and cayenne. Mix with your fingertips until well blended. Using your hands, shape the sausage mixture into 12–14 patties, each about 3 inches (7.5 cm) in diameter and ½ inch (12 mm) thick. (The patties can be made up to 1 day ahead, tightly covered, and refrigerated.)

In a large frying pan, warm the oil over medium-high heat. Working in batches, add the patties and cook until golden brown, 3–4 minutes. Turn and cook until the patties are golden brown on the second sides, 3–4 minutes. Transfer to paper towels to drain briefly, then serve.

serve with

Any egg dish you like and/or Breakfast Polenta with Maple Syrup and Blackberries (page 46) pairs well with the sausage. Accompany with fresh fruit and plenty of hot, strong coffee.

variation

If you own a sausage stuffer, you can stuff this sausage mixture into hog casings and tie off into any size links you like.

Nothing compares to the smoky, salty scent of bacon cooking. It conjures up the warmth of the morning table and the comforts of home. Here, the addition of a sweet maple glaze enhances a breakfast classic.

maple-glazed bacon

12 thick slices
applewood-smoked
bacon

2 Tbsp pure
maple syrup

½ tsp coarsely ground
black pepper

serves 6

Preheat the oven to 400°F (200°C). Spread the bacon in a single layer on a large baking sheet. Bake until the bacon is barely crisp and browned, 15–20 minutes. Carefully drain off and discard the fat from the baking sheet.

Brush 1 Tbsp of the maple syrup over the bacon strips and sprinkle with half of the pepper. Bake until the bacon is glazed and shiny, about 2½ minutes. Remove from the oven and, using tongs, turn the slices. Brush with the remaining 1 Tbsp syrup and sprinkle with the remaining pepper. Bake until glazed and shiny, about 2 minutes. Transfer the bacon to a platter. Let stand for 2–3 minutes. The bacon will firm up and become extra-crispy. Serve warm.

serve with

Pull out all the stops and serve up Jam-Filled Sweet Crepes (page 28) and a rich and indulgent egg dish, such as Mushroom Omelet with Parmesan and Thyme (page 71).

variation

You can use honey in place of the maple syrup. You can also experiment with different kinds of peppers (such as white or Sichuan) or pure chile powders (such as cayenne or chipotle).

roasted rosemary potatoes

1½ lb (750 g) small red potatoes, each about 1 inch (2.5 cm) in diameter, unpeeled

2 Tbsp extra-virgin olive oil

2–3 tsp salt

1 tsp freshly ground pepper

2 Tbsp minced fresh rosemary

serves 4–6

Preheat the oven to 350°F (180°C). Place the potatoes in a shallow baking dish just large enough to hold them snugly in a single layer. Drizzle with the oil and turn to coat well. Season generously with salt and pepper. Sprinkle with the rosemary and turn again to coat.

Roast the potatoes, turning once or twice, until the skins wrinkle and the potatoes can be easily pierced with a fork, about 1¼ hours.

Transfer the potatoes to a bowl and serve hot or at room temperature.

serve with

Roasted potatoes are one of the easiest and most delicious ways to add starch to a menu—and leaves the cook free to prepare a well-matched main dish that requires last-minute attention, like Steak and Eggs (page 96).

corn fritters

4 ears corn, white, yellow, or a mixture

¼ yellow onion, grated

¼ cup (1½ oz/45 g) all-purpose flour

½ tsp baking powder

¼ tsp sea salt

¼ tsp freshly ground pepper

1 large egg, lightly beaten

3 oz (90 g) Teleme cheese, cut into small cubes

Olive oil for frying

serves 4

Hold each ear of corn upright, base down, in a shallow bowl. Using a sharp knife, cut straight down between the kernels and the cob, freeing the kernels and rotating the ear a quarter turn after each cut. Transfer the corn kernels to a deep bowl. Add the onion, flour, baking powder, salt, and pepper and stir to mix. Add the egg and cheese and mix well.

Line a platter with paper towels. Pour oil to a depth of a scant ¼ inch (6 mm) into a large frying pan and heat over medium-high heat. When the oil begins to shimmer, carefully drop heaping teaspoonfuls of the corn mixture into the pan, spacing them about 1 inch (2.5 cm) apart. Using a spatula, gently press on the fritters and fry until golden brown on the first sides, about 2 minutes. Turn and fry until golden brown on the second sides, about 1 minute. Transfer the fritters to the towel–lined platter to drain. Repeat to cook the remaining corn mixture, adding more oil and reducing the heat if necessary.

Season with salt and serve hot or warm.

serve with

These fritters benefit from last-minute frying to maintain maximum crispness. Pair them with menu elements that can be prepared mostly ahead of time, such as a frittata, or require almost no last-minute prep, like granola with sliced fruit or Baked Eggs with Spinach and Cream (page 79).

buttermilk angel biscuits

2½ cups (12½ oz/
390 g) all-purpose
flour

2 Tbsp sugar

1 tsp baking powder

½ tsp baking soda

½ tsp salt

1 tsp quick-rise yeast

4 Tbsp (2 oz/60 g)
cold unsalted butter,
cut into cubes, plus
room-temperature
butter for serving

¼ cup (2 oz/60 g) cold
vegetable shortening,
cut into cubes

1 cup (8 fl oz/250 ml)
buttermilk

Honey or jam
for serving

serves 4

In a bowl, sift together the flour, sugar, baking powder, baking soda, and salt. Stir in the yeast. Using a pastry blender or 2 knives, cut the 4 Tbsp butter and the shortening into the dry ingredients just until the mixture forms coarse crumbs about the size of peas. Add the buttermilk and stir with a fork just until combined.

Shape the dough into a ball. Lightly butter a large bowl. Add the dough and turn to coat with the butter. Cover the bowl tightly with plastic wrap. Let the dough rise in a warm spot until it doubles in bulk, about 1¼ hours. (The dough can be refrigerated for up to 2 days before baking. Shape into a thick disk, close in a resealable plastic bag, and refrigerate. Punch down every 12 hours or so. Remove from the refrigerator 1 hour before shaping and baking.)

Preheat the oven to 425°F (220°C). Line a baking sheet with parchment paper.

Punch down the dough, then turn out onto a floured work surface. Pat into a 10-by-5-inch (25-by-13-cm) rectangle about ¾ inch (2 cm) thick. Cut into ten 2-inch (5-cm) squares. Place 1 inch (2.5 cm) apart on the prepared sheet.

Bake until golden brown, 17–20 minutes. Serve the biscuits warm with butter and honey.

serve with

The most important partner for these old-style flaky biscuits is good butter, slightly softened and applied with a liberal hand. Ham—whole, for slicing, or sizzled ham steaks—is another great match. Be sure to offer some fruit to add color and freshness to this delightfully retro menu.

cheese grits

3 large eggs

1 cup (8 fl oz/250 ml) whole milk

1 tsp salt

¾ cup (4 oz/125 g) grits

1 cup (4 oz/125 g) shredded white Cheddar cheese

1 cup (4 oz/125 g) shredded sharp Cheddar cheese

½ cup (1½ oz/45 g) minced green onions, white and light green parts

Freshly ground pepper

serves 4–6

Preheat the oven to 325°F (165°C). Butter a 2-qt (2-l) baking dish. In a bowl, whisk together the eggs and milk until well blended.

In a saucepan, combine 2 cups (16 fl oz/500 ml) water and the salt and bring to a boil over medium-high heat. Slowly stir in the grits. Reduce the heat to low, cover, and cook, stirring often, until the grits are soft and the water is absorbed, about 20 minutes. Remove from the heat and let stand, covered, for 5 minutes to thicken.

Add the egg mixture to the hot grits, and whisk until blended. Whisk in about three-fourths of each cheese and the green onions. Season with pepper and mix well. Pour the grits into the prepared dish and sprinkle with the remaining cheese.

Bake until the edges are brown and a toothpick inserted into the center comes out clean, about 20 minutes. Serve hot.

serve with

Grits are often served straight from the saucepan, but here they are baked, allowing the cook to concentrate on a dish that requires hands-on attention just before serving. Shrimp and sausage are traditional partners, and it would be nice to include a sweet and fruity element on this menu. Blackberry Coffee Cake (page 35) is a great choice.

spicy vegetable hash

1½ lb (750 g) orange-fleshed sweet potatoes, peeled and cut into small cubes

1½ lb (750 g) Yukon gold potatoes, peeled and cut into small cubes

2 Tbsp olive oil

1 yellow onion, chopped

1 red bell pepper, seeded and chopped

1 jalapeño chile, seeded and minced

1 cup (6 oz/185 g) fresh or thawed frozen corn kernels

1½ tsp ground cumin

3 Tbsp chopped fresh cilantro, plus more for garnish

Salt and freshly ground pepper

Plain yogurt for serving

Lime wedges for serving

serves 4–6

Preheat the oven to 400°F (200°C). Lightly oil a large rimmed baking sheet. Place all the potatoes on the prepared sheet. Drizzle with 1 Tbsp of the oil, toss to coat the potatoes, and spread in an even layer. Roast for 30 minutes. Turn the potatoes and continue roasting until lightly browned and tender, about 15 minutes. Keep warm.

Meanwhile, in a large frying pan, heat the remaining 1 Tbsp oil over medium heat. Add the onion, bell pepper, and jalapeño, and cook, stirring occasionally, until the vegetables are tender, about 10 minutes. Stir in the corn and cook until heated through, about 3 minutes. Stir in the cumin and cook until fragrant, about 30 seconds. Add the potatoes and the 3 Tbsp cilantro and stir to combine. Season with salt and pepper.

Spoon the hash into bowls. Top each serving with a dollop of yogurt and a sprinkle of cilantro. Serve with the lime wedges.

serve with

There is a south-of-the-border sensibility at work in this chunky and colorful hash, so start with Huevos Rancheros (page 85), and add refreshing Raspberry-Mint Agua Frescas (page 159). For a sweet note, choose guaranteed-to-please Coffee Cake Muffins (page 42).

variation

If you wish, top each serving of hash with a poached or fried egg (page 64–65).

With its clear, vegetable-forward Mediterranean flavors, this attractive and filling side adds color to your table and will go beautifully with any egg dish or with pancakes.

summer vegetable stacks

4 small eggplants, cut lengthwise into 3 slices

2 red bell peppers, seeded and cut lengthwise into quarters

¼ cup (2 fl oz/60 ml) olive oil, plus more for drizzling

2 Tbsp balsamic vinegar

1 tsp salt

½ tsp freshly ground pepper

8 large tomato slices

2–3 balls fresh mozzarella cheese, preferably buffalo's milk, cut into 8 slices

Handful of torn fresh basil leaves

serves 4

Place the eggplants and bell peppers in a bowl. Add the ¼ cup oil, vinegar, salt, and pepper. Turn several times and let stand for 30–60 minutes, turning once or twice. Prepare a charcoal or gas grill for direct-heat grilling over medium-high heat.

Arrange the eggplant slices and bell pepper quarters on the grill rack or in a single layer in a grilling basket. Cook until the vegetables are lightly charred, 6–7 minutes for the eggplants and about 4 minutes for the peppers. Turn and cook until browned and charred on the second sides. The timing will be about the same. Transfer the eggplant slices to a platter. Seal the peppers in a resealable plastic bag and let cool. Peel away the charred skin.

To assemble each stack, place a tomato slice on each plate, then top with a cheese slice, an eggplant slice, and a bell pepper quarter, seasoning the layers with salt and pepper. Repeat the layers, then top the stack with an eggplant slice. Drizzle with olive oil. Garnish with the basil leaves and serve.

serve with

Start things off with Lemon-Ricotta Pancakes with Compote (page 25), and tall tumblers of Amalfi Lemonade (page 162). Round out the menu with Swiss Chard, Onion, and Cheese Frittata (page 74).

Drinks

There is something wonderful
about being able to transform
a firm piece of bright-colored
fruit, fresh from the market or
a local tree, into a tall glass
of refreshing juice.

fresh fruit juices

california citrus juice

Choose from Valencia, navel, blood oranges, or white or pink grapefruits, or tangerines—or, make a mixture of several citrus fruits. Chill a juice pitcher in the refrigerator (keep the fruit refrigerated too, if possible). Microwave the fruits on high for 5 seconds only, to begin breaking down the membranes (this will yield more juice). Halve each fruit crosswise and cut a very shallow cross in the cut sides of each half. Juice the halves in a sturdy citrus juicer, then refrigerate the juice until just before serving time. Garnish the pitcher with a sprig or two of fresh mint, lemon balm, or lemon verbena.

fall fruit juice

If you have an extractor-style juicer, you're probably familiar with all the wonderful options for non-citrus-fruit and vegetable juices. One of my favorites is apple-pear-cranberry: Stem, peel, core, and chop the apples and pears roughly, using the amounts recommended by the juicer manufacturer. Process the fruit in the juicer as directed. Transfer the juice to a chilled pitcher and stir in 2–4 Tbsp of unsweetened store-bought cranberry juice; chill until serving time. Pour into tall glasses half filled with ice, and scatter just a few grains of Chinese five-spice powder or ground cinnamon on the top of each serving.

sparkling ginger lemonade

½ cup (2 oz/60 g) peeled and
thinly sliced fresh ginger

¾ cup (6 fl oz/180 ml) fresh lemon juice

¾ cup (6 oz/185 g) sugar,
plus more as needed

2½ cups (20 fl oz/625 ml)
well-chilled sparkling water

Ice cubes

6 lemon slices for garnish

6 strips crystallized ginger
for garnish

In a nonreactive saucepan, bring 4 cups
(32 fl oz/1 l) water to a boil over high heat.
Add the ginger slices, cover, and remove
from the heat. Let stand for 5 minutes. For a
stronger ginger flavor, let stand for an additional
5–10 minutes. Strain the ginger infusion through
a fine-mesh sieve into a glass jar, cover, and
refrigerate until well chilled.

Have ready 6 tall glasses. Pour the lemon juice
into a large pitcher. Gradually add the ¾ cup
sugar, whisking constantly until dissolved. Stir
in the sparkling water. Add more sugar to taste.

Fill the glasses with ice cubes. Pour in equal
amounts of the ginger infusion and the lemon
mixture, and stir well. Garnish each glass with
a lemon slice and a crystallized ginger strip,
and serve.

serves 6

mango lassi

2 ripe mangoes

1 tsp fresh lemon juice

2–4 Tbsp sugar or honey

2 cups (16 oz/500 g)
nonfat plain yogurt

1 cup (8 oz/250 g) ice cubes

Stand 1 mango on one of its narrow sides,
with the stem end facing you. Using a sharp
knife, and positioning it about 1 inch (2.5 cm)
from the stem, cut down the length of the fruit,
just brushing the pit. Repeat on the other side
of the pit. Peel away the skin from the 2 slabs
of flesh and chop the flesh coarsely. Repeat
with the second mango.

Have ready 4 tall glasses. In a blender, combine
the mango, lemon juice, sugar to taste, yogurt,
and ice. Blend until frothy and smooth. Pour
into the glasses and serve.

serves 4

honey-tangerine fizz

3 cups (24 fl oz/750 ml)
fresh tangerine juice

Juice of 1 lemon

¼ cup (3 oz/90 g) orange blossom honey

Crushed ice

2 cups (16 fl oz/500 ml) lemon- or
raspberry-flavored sparkling water

Raspberries for garnish

Have ready 4–6 tumblers. In a large pitcher, combine
the tangerine juice, lemon juice, and honey. Stir
vigorously until the honey is completely dissolved.
Add about 2 cups (8 oz/250 g) crushed ice and
slowly pour in the sparkling water. Stir gently.

Fill the glasses with crushed ice and pour in the
tangerine fizz. Garnish each drink with a raspberry
or two and serve.

serves 4–6

fruit smoothie

2 ripe bananas, peeled and frozen

2 cups (12 oz/375 g) pineapple, peach,
or mango cubes, frozen

1 cup (4 oz/125 g) raspberries, blueberries,
or sliced strawberries, frozen

½ cup (4 oz/125 g) vanilla yogurt

1½ cups (12 fl oz/375 ml) fresh orange juice

Have ready 4 tumblers. In a blender, combine
the bananas, pineapple, berries, yogurt, and
orange juice. Process until thick and creamy.
Pour into the glasses and serve.

serves 4

raspberry-mint agua fresca

½ cup (3½ oz/105 g)
superfine sugar

22 raspberries

22 fresh mint leaves, plus
4 sprigs for garnish

Ice cubes

Have ready 4 tumblers. In a saucepan, combine the sugar
and ½ cup (4 fl oz/125 ml) water. Bring to a simmer
over medium-low heat, stirring to dissolve the sugar.
Remove the sugar syrup from the heat and let cool.

In a blender, combine 18 of the raspberries, the mint
leaves, and the sugar syrup and process until a smooth
purée forms. Strain the purée through a fine-mesh sieve
into a pitcher. You should have about ⅔ cup (5 fl oz/
160 ml). Add 1⅓ cups (11 fl oz/340 ml) water.

Fill the glasses with ice and pour in the raspberry
mixture. Garnish with the mint sprigs and the
remaining raspberries, and serve.

serves 4

michelada

1 Tbsp plus 1 tsp coarse sea salt

2 tsp pure chile powder

6 limes

Ice cubes

4 tsp Worcestershire sauce

Hot-pepper sauce to taste

4 bottles (12 fl oz/375 ml each) Mexican beer, such as Dos Equis or Pacifico

Have ready 4 tall glasses or tumblers. Spread the salt and chile powder on a small, flat plate. Cut 2 of the limes into 4 wedges each. Run 1 lime wedge around the rim of each glass to moisten it and then dip the rim into the chile salt to coat it evenly. Reserve the remaining 4 lime wedges for garnish.

Juice the remaining 4 limes; you should have about 8 Tbsp (4 fl oz/125 ml) lime juice.

Fill each glass with several ice cubes. Add 2 Tbsp of the lime juice, 1 tsp of the Worcestershire sauce, and a dash or two of hot-pepper sauce to each glass. Pour 1 beer into each glass and stir gently. Garnish with a lime wedge and serve.

serves 4

balsamic bloody mary

Ice cubes

1 cup (8 fl oz/250 ml) vodka

2 cups (16 fl oz/500 ml) tomato juice

1 Tbsp balsamic vinegar, preferably aged

2 tsp prepared horseradish

2 tsp Worcestershire sauce

Hot-pepper sauce to taste

Juice of 1 lemon

Juice of 1 lime

Freshly ground pepper

4 celery stalks

4 green olives

4 peperoncini

Fill 4 tall glasses with ice cubes. In a large pitcher, combine the vodka, tomato juice, vinegar, horseradish, Worcestershire sauce, hot-pepper sauce, and lemon and lime juices. Season with pepper and stir well to combine.

Pour into the glasses. Garnish each glass with a celery stalk and a green olive and peperoncini speared on a cocktail pick, and serve.

serves 4

For a winter or holiday brunch, I like to serve sparkling cocktails and hot chocolate. Both are good with savory snacks, like slices of whole-wheat toast topped with European-style butter, tea biscuits, or shortbread.

grapefruit-prosecco sparkler

4 Tbsp (2 fl oz/60 ml) orange liqueur

8 Tbsp (4 fl oz/125 ml) fresh pink grapefruit juice

2 cups (16 fl oz/500 ml) Prosecco

4 pink grapefruit wedges for garnish

Pour 1 Tbsp orange liqueur, 2 Tbsp pink grapefruit juice, and ⅓ cup (4 fl oz/125 ml) Prosecco into each of 4 chilled Champagne flutes or wineglasses. Stir briefly.

Garnish each flute with a grapefruit wedge and serve.

serves 4

amalfi lemonade

8 lemon verbena leaves, plus sprigs for garnish

½ cup (4 oz/125 g) sugar

1¼ cups (10 fl oz/310 ml) fresh lemon juice

Ice cubes

2 lemons, thinly sliced, for garnish

In a saucepan, bring 2 cups (16 fl oz/500 ml) water to a boil. Place the 8 lemon verbena leaves in a heatproof measuring cup and pour in the boiling water. Add the sugar and stir until dissolved. Let stand for 10 minutes. Strain through a fine-mesh sieve into a bowl and refrigerate for at least 30 minutes.

Pour the lemon verbena syrup into a pitcher. Pour in 4 cups (32 fl oz/1 l) water and stir in the lemon juice.

Fill tall glasses with ice cubes. Pour in the lemonade. Garnish each glass with a lemon verbena sprig and a lemon slice, and serve.

serves 6–8

blood orange mimosa

4 Tbsp (2 fl oz/60 ml) orange liqueur

8 Tbsp (4 fl oz/125 ml) fresh
blood orange juice

2 cups (16 fl oz/500 ml) Champagne
or sparkling white wine

1 slice blood orange, quartered,
for garnish

Pour 1 Tbsp orange liqueur, 2 Tbsp blood orange juice, and ½ cup (4 fl oz/125 ml) Champagne into each of 4 chilled Champagne flutes or wineglasses. Stir briefly to mix.

Garnish each flute with an orange quarter, and serve.

serves 4

peach bellini

2 ripe peaches, peeled, halved, and pitted

1 Tbsp superfine sugar, or to taste

1 tsp fresh lemon juice, or to taste

1 bottle (24 fl oz/750 ml) Champagne,
Prosecco, or dry sparkling wine, chilled

Coarsely chop the peaches. In a blender, process the peaches to a smooth purée. Taste and add sugar and/or lemon juice if needed; the purée should be sweet but not overly sweet.

Fill 4 Champagne flutes about one-third full with the peach purée. Slowly fill the flutes with the Champagne. Stir briefly and serve.

serves 4

cantaloupe agua fresca

4 cups (1¼ lb/625 g) cubed very ripe cantaloupe

½ cup (4 fl oz/125 ml) fresh lime juice

⅓ cup (3 oz/90 g) sugar

1¼ cups (10 fl oz/310 ml) tequila

Crushed ice

Lime slices for garnish

Thin cantaloupe wedges for garnish

In a blender, combine the cubed melon, lime juice, and sugar. Process until the melon is completely liquefied and the mixture is smooth. Transfer to a pitcher and add 3 cups (24 fl oz/750 ml) water and the tequila. Stir to mix well.

Fill glasses with crushed ice and pour in the melon mixture. Garnish each glass with a lime slice and a melon wedge, and serve.

serves 4–6

Brunch offers the opportunity to enjoy a daytime drink. Vary your offerings with the seasons and different fresh ingredients. In summer, sangrias and agua frescas are cool and thirst-quenching.

summer fruit rosé sangria

1 bottle (24 fl oz/750 ml) Provençal rosé

1¼ cups (10 fl oz/310 ml) white cranberry juice

1 pt (8 oz/250 g) raspberries

1 pt (8 oz/250 g) blackberries or pitted cherries

1 nectarine, thinly sliced

1 white peach, thinly sliced

Ice cubes

In a pitcher, combine the rosé, cranberry juice, raspberries, blackberries, nectarine, and peach. Stir well. Refrigerate until chilled and the flavors are blended, about 2 hours.

Fill glasses with ice cubes, pour in the sangria, and serve.

serves 6–8

ramos fizz

¾ cup (6 fl oz/180 ml) gin

¼ cup (2 fl oz/60 ml) heavy cream

Juice of 4 lemons

4 large egg whites

8 drops orange flower water

¼ cup (2 oz/60 g) superfine sugar

Ice cubes

Chill 4 tall glasses. In a blender, combine the gin, cream, lemon juice, egg whites, orange flower water, and sugar, and process until smooth and frothy. Add enough ice to fill the blender three-fourths full. Remove the blender canister from the base, cover the canister tightly, and shake gently to cool the drink. Strain through a fine-mesh sieve into the glasses and serve.

Note: This recipe calls for raw egg whites. While the incidence of bacteria in raw eggs is rare, anyone with a compromised immune system should use caution.

serves 4

cucumber-chile agua fresca

10 cucumbers, peeled, seeded, and cut into chunks

1 cup (8 fl oz/250 ml) fresh lime juice

2 Tbsp agave nectar or honey

½ serrano chile, seeded and minced

Sea salt

2 cups (16 fl oz/500 ml) silver tequila

Ice cubes

In a blender, working in batches if necessary, combine 4½ cups (36 fl oz/1.1 l) water with the cucumbers, lime juice, agave nectar, and chile. Add a generous pinch of salt and purée until smooth. Strain through a fine-mesh sieve into a pitcher. Add the tequila and chill in the refrigerator for at least 1 hour.

Fill glasses with ice cubes, pour in the cucumber mixture, and serve.

serves 6–8

watermelon-lime agua fresca

8 cups (2½ lb/1.25 kg) seedless watermelon chunks

1 cup (8 fl oz/250 ml) fresh lime juice

½ cup (4 oz/125 g) sugar

2 cups (16 fl oz/500 ml) gold tequila

½ cup (4 fl oz/125 ml) Grand Marnier

Ice cubes

In a blender, working in batches if necessary, combine 4 cups (32 fl oz/1 l) water with the watermelon, lime juice, and sugar. Blend until completely liquid and frothy. Transfer to a pitcher, add the tequila and Grand Marnier, and stir to combine.

Fill glasses with ice cubes, pour in the watermelon mixture, and serve.

serves 6–8

spiced iced coffee

4½ cups (36 fl oz/1.1 l) freshly brewed hot coffee

6 Tbsp (3 oz/90 g) sugar

3 Tbsp unsweetened Dutch-process cocoa powder

2 cinnamon sticks

6 whole cloves

4 strips orange zest, each about 3 inches (7.5 cm) long by 1 inch (2.5 cm) wide

Ice cubes

Milk or half-and-half for serving

In a heatproof bowl, combine the coffee, sugar, and cocoa powder. Stir thoroughly to dissolve the sugar and cocoa. Add the cinnamon sticks and cloves. Twist each piece of orange zest to release the essential oils, then add to the hot liquid. Let the coffee stand for 1 hour, stirring occasionally, to infuse the flavors.

Strain the coffee into a large pitcher. Cover and refrigerate until very cold, about 2 hours.

Fill tumblers with ice cubes. Stir the coffee and pour over the ice until the glasses are three-fourths full. Fill the glasses with milk, stir well, and serve.

serves 6

whipped hot chocolate

2 cups (16 fl oz/500 ml) low-fat or whole milk

4 tsp unsweetened Dutch-process cocoa powder

4 tsp sugar

8 oz (250 g) bittersweet chocolate, finely chopped or grated

¼ tsp salt

¼ tsp ground cinnamon

Brandy for serving (optional)

Vanilla ice cream for serving (optional)

In a small saucepan, combine the milk, cocoa powder, and sugar. Heat over medium heat, whisking until the sugar dissolves and the mixture is warmed through. Add the chocolate, salt, and cinnamon, and continue whisking vigorously until the mixture is frothy, smooth, and very warm.

Pour into coffee cups or mugs. Add brandy or ice cream, or both, if using, and serve.

serves 4

lemon verbena and mint tisane

1 bunch fresh lemon verbena sprigs

1 bunch fresh mint

Sugar for serving (optional)

Have ready 2 mugs. If desired, set aside 2 lemon verbena sprigs for garnish. Put the remaining lemon verbena sprigs and the mint in a teapot. In a saucepan, bring 3 cups (24 fl oz/750 ml) water to a boil over high heat. Pour into the teapot and let the tisane steep until it reaches the desired strength, 3–5 minutes.

Pour through a tea strainer or fine-mesh sieve into the mugs. Garnish each mug with a lemon verbena sprig, if using, and serve. Pass the sugar at the table, if desired.

serves 2

chai latte

1 cinnamon stick, about 1½ inches (4 cm)

4 green cardamom pods

4 black cardamom pods

10 whole cloves

2 peppercorns

5 thin slices peeled fresh ginger

⅔ cup (5 fl oz/160 ml) whole milk

2 Tbsp sugar

4 tsp Darjeeling tea leaves

In a saucepan, combine the cinnamon stick, cardamom pods, cloves, peppercorns, and ginger slices. Add 1½ cups (12 fl oz/375 ml) water and bring to a boil over medium heat. Cover, reduce the heat to low, and simmer until the liquid becomes aromatic, about 10 minutes.

Add the milk and sugar and bring to a simmer over medium heat. Stir in the tea leaves, remove from the heat, cover, and let stand until the chai reaches the desired strength, 3–5 minutes.

Have ready 2 mugs. If you have an espresso machine, steam and froth half of the chai according to the manufacturer's instructions. Return the chai to the pan. Pour the chai through a tea strainer or fine-mesh sieve into the mugs, top with the foam, and serve. Alternatively, reheat the chai over medium heat before serving.

serves 2

Tea has caused rebellions, disrupted cultures, and once helped drive a handful of Asian economies. Today's tea choices are abundant, nontraditional, and ravishlingly beautiful—as well as deeply satisfying.

homemade teas

honey-lemon tea punch

Combine 4 Tbsp loose black tea leaves and 4 cups (32 fl oz/1 l) water in a teapot or heat-proof jug and let steep for 5 minutes. Stir in ⅔ cup (8 oz/ 250 g) honey and the juice from 2 large lemons. When the tea is cool, strain it into a pitcher or punch bowl filled with crushed ice. Add 1 cup (8 fl oz/250 ml) sparkling water and a handful of fresh mint sprigs and serve. *serves 6*

spiced tea

In a saucepan, combine 3 cups (24 fl oz/ 750 ml) water, 4 whole cloves, 1 cinnamon stick, and 4 allspice berries. Bring to a simmer, cook for 10 minutes, then remove from the heat. Add 1 Tbsp fresh lemon juice. Place 1 tsp black tea leaves in a sieve and pour the spiced hot water over the tea leaves into a teapot or directly into tea cups. Sweeten with honey or agave nectar as desired. *serves 3–4*

apple-orange tea

Quarter and core 2 red apples. Quarter 1 orange. In a saucepan, combine the fruit quarters, 1 cinnamon stick, 2 whole cloves, 4 Tbsp black tea leaves, and 4 cups (32 fl oz/1 l) water. Bring to a boil over medium- high heat, then remove from the heat and let stand for 30 minutes. Strain into a pitcher or jug, pressing on the fruit to extract all the flavor. Let cool to room temperature, then serve over ice or reheat in a saucepan to serve warm. Sweeten with sugar or honey as desired. *serves 4–6*

ginger-mint tea

In a teapot or heatproof jug, combine ½ cup (2 oz/60 g) peeled and thinly sliced fresh ginger, a handful of fresh mint or lemon verbena sprigs, and 6 cups (48 fl oz/1.5 l) boiling water. Let steep for 5 minutes. Serve hot or over ice. *serves 6*

index

weldon**owen**

415 Jackson Street, Suite 200, San Francisco, CA 94111
www.weldonowen.com

LET'S DO BRUNCH

Conceived and produced by Weldon Owen, Inc.
In collaboration with Williams-Sonoma, Inc.
3250 Van Ness Avenue, San Francisco, CA 94109

A WELDON OWEN PRODUCTION

Printed and bound in China by Toppan-Leefung

First printed in 2012
10 9 8 7 6 5 4 3 2 1

Library of Congress Control Number: 2012952912

ISBN 13: 978-1-61628-542-5
ISBN 10: 1-61628-542-7

Weldon Owen is a division of
BONNIER

WELDON OWEN, INC.

CEO and President Terry Newell
VP, Sales and Marketing Amy Kaneko
Director of Finance Mark Perrigo

VP and Publisher Hannah Rahill
Associate Publisher Amy Marr

Creative Director Emma Boys
Senior Designer Lauren Charles

Production Director Chris Hemesath
Production Manager Michelle Duggan

Photographer Ray Kachatorian
Food Stylist Alison Attenborough
Prop Stylist Leigh Noe

ACKNOWLEDGMENTS

Weldon Owen wishes to thank the following people for their generous support in producing this book: Carolyn Cuykendall, Judith Dunham, Anna Grace, Max Gray, Rachel Lopez Metzger, Elizabeth Parson, Kevin Scott, Sharon Silva, and Jen Stark